LIVING PLANET

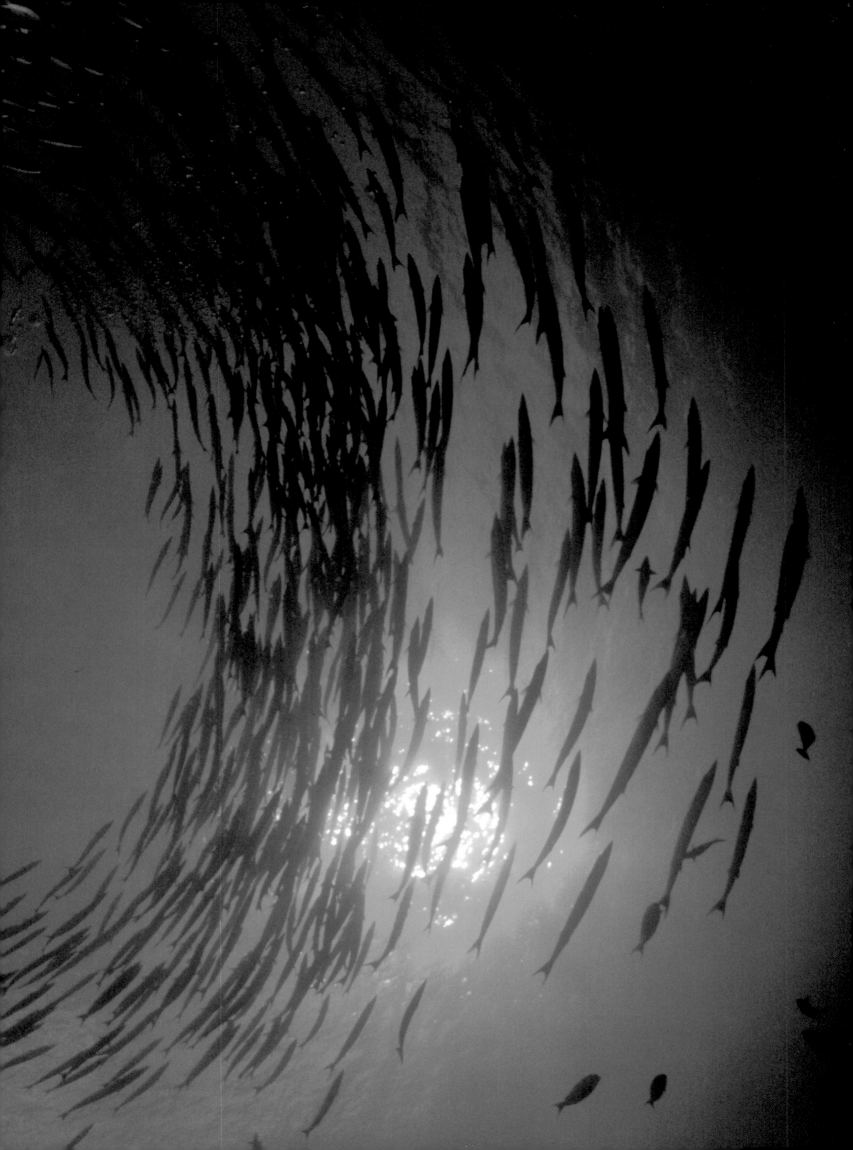

LIVING

WWF
WORLD WILDLIFE FUND

PLANET

PRESERVING EDENS OF THE EARTH

Photographs by
Frans Lanting, Galen Rowell & David Doubilet

Text by
Noel Grove

Foreword by
Walter Cronkite

Produced by
Jennifer Barry Design

CROWN PUBLISHERS, INC.
NEW YORK

The unsung heroes of this story are the thousands of committed conservationists living and working throughout the Global 200 ecoregions celebrated in the following pages. Around the world they fight the battles to preserve the Earth's wondrous biodiversity as a legacy for our children. To them, World Wildlife Fund gratefully dedicates this book.

Living Planet® is a registered trademark of WWF-International.

Copyright © 1999 by World Wildlife Fund
All photographs credited to Frans Lanting copyright © 1999 by Frans Lanting; www.lanting.com
All photographs credited to Galen Rowell copyright © 1999 by Galen Rowell; www.mountainlight.com
All photographs credited to David Doubilet copyright © 1999 by David Doubilet; www.doubiletphoto.com

Published by Crown Publishers, Inc., 201 East 50th Street, New York, New York 10022. Member of the Crown Publishing Group.

Random House, Inc. New York, Toronto, London, Sydney, Auckland
www.randomhouse.com

CROWN is a trademark and the C & Sun Design are registered trademarks of Random House, Inc.

Printed in Hong Kong

Design by Jennifer Barry

Library of Congress Cataloging-in-Publication Data is available upon request.

ISBN 0-609-60466-x

10 9 8 7 6 5 4 3 2 1
First Edition

World Wildlife Fund
1250 24th Street NW, Washington, DC 20037
202-293-4800
www.worldwildlife.org

A royalty between 4% and 7% of the estimated retail price is received by WWF on all sales of this book.
These funds help support WWF's efforts to preserve the wild spaces and species of the Global 200.

Pages 2–3, *Papua New Guinea: Global 200 Ecoregion #210.* Pacific barracuda circle a diver near New Ireland, east of New Guinea. *Photographer: David Doubilet.* Pages 4–5, *Botswana: Global 200 Ecoregion #105.* African elephants plod toward a water hole during the dry season in the Okavango Delta. *Photographer: Frans Lanting.* Pages 6–7, *Papua New Guinea: Global 200 Ecoregion #210.* Clownfish hover in the tentacles of an anemone near Milne Bay. *Photographer: David Doubilet.* Pages 8–9, *California, U.S.A.: Global 200 Ecoregion #75.* Winter snow powders boulders in the Merced River at Gates of the Valley, Yosemite National Park. *Photographer: Galen Rowell.* Pages 10–11, *Borneo: Global 200 Ecoregion #40.* Fallen trees leave gaps in the canopy of a rain forest. *Photographer: Frans Lanting.* Pages 12–13, *Alaska, U.S.A.: Global 200 Ecoregion #141.* Alaskan brown bear lunges for a salmon at Brooks Falls in Katmai National Park. *Photographer: Galen Rowell.* Pages 14–15, *California, U.S.A.: Global 200 Ecoregion #74, #140.* Snow geese migrating southward alight on Tule Lake. *Photographer: Frans Lanting.* Pages 16–17, *French Polynesia: Global 200 Ecoregion #215.* Humpback whale and its newborn calf cruise near the surface of the South Pacific. *Photographer: David Doubilet.* Pages 18–19, *Antarctica: Global 200 Ecoregion #233.* Emperor penguins rear their downy chicks beside the Weddell Sea on the Riiser-Larsen Ice Shelf. *Photographer: Galen Rowell.* Page 24, *Washington D.C.:* A giant panda, symbol of the struggle to save vanishing wildlife, munches bamboo at the National Zoo. *Photographer: Frans Lanting.*

This book was printed entirely on recycled paper.

ACKNOWLEDGMENTS

Special thanks for the creation of this book go to Roger W. Sant, whose vision, leadership, and encouragement have guided and inspired World Wildlife Fund's Living Planet Campaign and the Global 200 Initiative.

WWF also wishes to acknowledge the contribution of the following: Drs. Eric Dinerstein and David Olson, who conceived the Global 200; Deborah Grovesnor, literary agent; Ayesha Pande, editor; Noel Grove, writer; and Jennifer Barry, book packager.

David Doubilet would like especially to thank the following people for their invaluable help and worldwide conservation aware-ness: his wife, Anne, and daughter Emily; Koji and Miyuki Nakamura in Japan; Yves Lefevre in French Polynesia; Gary Bell in Australia, Tasmania, and New Zealand; Dr. Gerard Wellington and Mauricio Handler in the Galápagos; David Fridman in the Red Sea; Jay Ireland in the Caymans.

Frans Lanting wishes to ac-knowledge the kind assistance and cooperation of the following people and organizations: Garo Batmanian, Mauro Giuntini, and the staff at WWF-Brasil; Cleber Alho; Denise Marçal Rambaldi and the Associação Mico-Leao-Dourado; Reserva Biogica de Poço das Antas; Eduardo Marcelino Ventura Veado, Jairo Vieira Gomes, and the staff at Estação Biologica de Caratinga at Fazenda Montes Claros; Marta Leitman and the staff at Jardim Botanico do Rio de Janeiro; Fernando Dutra; Raquel Werneck; Parque Nacional Serra dos Orgãos; Zalmio Cubas and the staff at Parque das Aves; Julio Gonchorosky and the staff at Parque Nacional do Iguaçu; Paulo Martins and Helisul; the staff at Frans Lanting

Inc., with special thanks to Mark Oatney and personal and professional gratitude to Christine Eckstrom.

Galen Rowell wishes to acknowledge Bruce Bunting and Mingma Norbu Sherpa of WWF-Nepal; Al Read, Jim Sano, Ang Tsering, and the staff at Geographic Expedi-tions; Ervin and Elena Skalamera; Bill Abbott, Ray Rodney, Jonathan Green, and the staff of Wilderness Travel; Luis Chard of Turismo Yamana, Chile; Rick Cook, Shannon Estanoz, Joe Lamonoco, and R.W. Freer of Everglades Outpost in the Florida Everglades; Tundra Tom Faess, Terry Elliot, and Dwayne Roberge in Canada's Northwest Territories; Eric Grandison of the Nisga'a tribe in British Columbia; Dave Cline and Margaret Williams in Alaska for WWF-Bering Sea; Jerry Grossman, Sharon Lebowitz, and Richard LoPinto of Nikon; Ryan Baldwin, Gary Crabbe, Chesley Crowell, and Barry Sundermeier of Mountain Light Photography, and particularly its president— my partner on so many Global 200 journeys—my wife, Barbara Cushman Rowell.

Jennifer Barry Design would like to thank and acknowledge the assistance of the following people who helped in the creation of this book: layout production assistant Kristen Wurz; Leslie Barry; Tom Johnson; copyeditor Blake Hallanan; proofreader Ken Della Penta; Jody and Shlomo Sela; publishing advisor Peter Beren; photographers Galen Rowell, Frans Lanting, and David Doubilet and their wives and office staffs; and special thanks to Tom McGuire and Jo Lynn Dorrance at WWF, and to editor Ayesha Pande of Crown Publishers.

FOREWORD

BY WALTER CRONKITE

Man is the enemy of the environment and Man is winning. Principally through his efforts, not always intentional, Earth is losing one hundred species of animals, plants, insects and fungi every day. Experts estimate that the world has lost one-third of its biological wealth over the past thirty years; that one in five species will become extinct in the next thirty years; that one in eight known species of plant is imperiled.

Earth already has lost two-thirds of its original forest cover and we are now losing what remains at an astounding rate of 1.3 acres per second. Almost 70 percent of the world's coral reefs, "rain forests of the sea," either have been destroyed or are endangered. All but two of the world's fifteen major fisheries are at the point of collapse.

The slaughter must cease. Only Man can declare an armistice.

Unless peace is achieved, this massive extinction crisis will pose a major threat to human beings themselves in the twenty-first century. A Harris survey of biologists across the nation showed that seven out of ten are so convinced.

We are attacking the environment with a multitude of high-powered, lethal weapons: pollution, deforestation, global warming, unregulated development, overconsumption of resources, destruction of habitat, to name a few of the more insidious.

There have been many alarms and much hand-wringing. And there are not a few valiant efforts at action. Almost exclusively they have concentrated on so-called "hot spots"—endangered areas of high species concentration.

World Wildlife Fund, however, has developed a new approach—a concentration on two hundred areas that collectively represent the broadest possible range of the Earth's most distinctive ecosystems. They are the places we must save to preserve a representative sampling of the diversity of life. Indeed, it is the conservationist's vision of Noah's ark.

This Global 200 campaign includes some of the glamorous, much publicized places like the tropical rain forests of Brazil and central Africa and the Atlantic and Pacific coral reefs. However, it also includes less well-known although no less spectacular places like the vast Siberian forest, the teeming waters of the Bering Sea, and the unique rivers and streams of the southeastern United States.

This exciting book takes us to many of these endangered areas targeted for salvation by WWF's armistice. It is that organization's hope that these images of nature's incredible beauty will help rally public support for the Global 200 objective—no less a goal than saving our planet.

As Harvard's world-renowned biologist Dr. Edward O. Wilson says: "World Wildlife Fund has exercised its impressive research capability to create the most comprehensive strategy to date for the conservation of the world's biodiversity."

INTRODUCTION

A LEGACY IN THE WILD

We occupy an extraordinary planet, a spherical garden teeming with life. Viewed from space, the Earth sparkles like a delicate blue-and-white marble cast among lifeless rocks. That marble represents a miracle in a barren solar system. Formed by cosmic debris, layered by lava, sculpted by ice, and robed in vegetation, our Earth is a landscape of infinite variety. Yet although our planet may appear lush and fertile, scientists tell us we are witnessing a series of extinctions different from any in human history—extinctions not just of species but of entire habitats and ecosystems. This is not a natural extinction crisis, such as the one that brought the age of dinosaurs to an end, but one that is caused by people.

Today, on average, more than an acre of forest disappears every second. Global warming, caused in large part by the rapid rate at which we burn coal, oil, and gas, is disturbing the migration of songbirds, causing the bleaching of coral reefs, and melting glaciers. Expanding human populations are degrading forests, savannas, wetlands, and rivers at a rate never experienced before. The species that inhabit them—including plants that heal and fish that feed millions of people—are losing ground too. If present trends continue, as many as one-fifth of all the plant and animal species alive could face extinction within thirty years.

Without immediate and strategic action, the web of life that has taken 4 billion years to evolve will tatter and unravel—with profound consequences for every living thing. Our very survival depends on the clean air and water, foodstuffs and building materials, healing medicines and climate moderation that only healthy natural ecosystems can provide.

With a new millennium at hand, World Wildlife Fund (WWF) has launched its Living Planet Campaign to safeguard the extraordinary abundance and diversity of life on this planet. This campaign will focus on preserving certain animal species in imminent danger of disappearing, such as tigers, rhinos, giant pandas, and whales, as well as seeking solutions to global threats such as degradation of forests, overfishing, climate change, and toxic pollution. The shining centerpiece of the Living Planet Campaign is the Global 200, a landmark effort to protect those places on Earth with the greatest biological wealth.

In an ideal world, conservation would mean saving every species and habitat on Earth, but given our limited resources, difficult choices must be made. WWF scientists wondered, if we cannot save all the pieces, how do we identify the regions most in need of conservation? To find the answer, they launched the most comprehensive assessment of biological diversity ever undertaken. As a result, they identified more than two hundred outstanding examples of the Earth's diverse terrestrial, freshwater, and marine habitats—areas where the planet's biota is most distinctive and rich, where its loss will be most severely felt, and where we must fight the hardest for conservation.

The concept is simple, yet profound: By conserving the broadest variety of the world's habitats, we can conserve the broadest variety of the world's species and most endangered wildlife, as well as higher expressions of life—whole communities and ecosystems. Regardless of where they are located, Global 200 ecoregions are all unique expressions of biological diversity, each with its own highly distinctive species, ecological processes, and evolutionary phenomena.

Consider, for example, the dry tropical forests on the Texas-sized island of Madagascar. Millennia of isolation from the African continent have given the island thousands of species found nowhere else on Earth, including some thirty species of lemur, two-thirds of the world's chameleons, and the angonoka tortoise, one of the world's most threatened reptiles. An astonishing 98 percent of Madagascar's land mammals exist nowhere else on Earth, and many of them inhabit the forests in the western part of the island—forests rapidly being depleted by an expanding human population and logging for fuelwood. Already, thousands of acres have been cleared for agriculture or pasture, and unchecked burning of the surrounding savannas is eating away at the few remaining forest fragments.

The Chihuahuan Desert in the southwestern United States and northern Mexico had early explorers marveling at its lush native grasses, forest-lined rivers and streams, rich wetlands, and free-roaming populations of pronghorn, desert bighorn sheep, and Mexican wolf. In terms of biological diversity, this region outstrips many better-known North American places: it boasts more mammal species than Greater Yellowstone, more bird species than the Florida Everglades, and more plant species than the forests of the Pacific Northwest. About 350 species of cacti, many of them confined to a single valley or hillside, can be found here, along with some 250 species of butterfly. Today, the beautiful and sleek Mexican wolf is nearly extinct in the wild; grasslands have given way to irrigated farm fields; wetlands and riverbank forests have

fallen victim to overgrazing, erosion, and water diversion; and aquatic habitats vital for the survival of wildlife are being destroyed.

To protect these and other vast ecological treasures, WWF had to formulate a perspective large enough to see the big picture—a picture that presents enormous challenges: How does one balance people's livelihood with the need to conserve wildlife and wildlands? How does one integrate social and political concerns so that conservation progress will endure? And how does one forge cooperative alliances between governments, across political boundaries?

With these challenges in mind, WWF has already successfully launched projects in many of the Global 200 ecoregions. In Madagascar, for example, it has forged partnerships with the national government and local communities to manage the Beza Mahafaly and Zombitze Vohibasia national parks; it is conducting surveys of the effects of population growth and migration on the region's wildlife; and to help slow the rampant clearing of Madagascar's forests triggered by the need for fuelwood, WWF is helping residents design and build fuel-efficient woodstoves.

To protect the precious aquatic habitats of the Chihuahuan Desert, WWF is working with local conservationists and landowners in Mexico and the United States to help create a management plan for the area's freshwater springs. WWF has also called on a group of Mexican and American scientists to map out strategies for protection of such key areas as the Davis Mountains of Texas, the Sky Islands of Arizona, and the desert scrub communities of the Meseta Central.

In Kayan Mentarang National Park on Borneo, a group of Bornean scientists, students, and government officials, brought together and coordinated by WWF, went to live among the native people for months to learn from them how to use the resources of the forest without destroying it. In the Galápagos Islands, home to such unique species as the marine iguana and the giant tortoise, WWF has teamed with Ecuadorean ecologists to free the islands of introduced species including dogs, cats, rats, and goats that prey on the native wildlife and compete for their food.

In Brazil, WWF is working closely with the government to monitor the building of a giant waterworks project that has the potential to devastate the world's largest wetland in the Pantanal. WWF program officers are also working with Brazilian researchers to save the golden lion tamarin from extinction. Its habitat, the Atlantic Coastal forest, is dwindling rapidly from continuing human encroachment.

The Klamath-Siskiyou Forests of California and Oregon are renowned for their extraordinary biological diversity. In addition to harboring the largest concentration of wild and scenic rivers in the United States, this Global 200 ecoregion is also home to a variety of rare animal species, including the northern goshawk, the bald eagle, and the mountain lion. Seventeen different conifer species have been found in one valley within a single square mile. But excessive logging, mining, and grazing have threatened this diversity. WWF is working with the Klamath-Siskiyou Alliance, business interests, and community leaders to identify the region's most outstanding conservation areas, set conservation priorities, and promote long-term economic development that sustains, rather than strains, natural resources. WWF's work with private landowners dovetails with continuing efforts to certify and promote timber from environmentally sound logging operations.

The secluded valleys of the Eastern Himalayas have the world's most diverse temperate forests, the world's tallest grasslands, and the highest densities of tigers and rhinos in Asia. Other rare animals that inhabit this region include Asian elephants, red pandas, golden langurs, takins, and snow leopards. The remarkable diversity of wildlife in this region is increasingly threatened by an impoverished and rapidly growing human population. Demand for firewood and fodder destroys local forests; overgrazing imperils grasslands and meadows; and poaching is a continued threat to already endangered species. WWF is helping local communities to manage their own natural resources: In one such project, local villages are managing tourism to the Annapurna Conservation Area and reducing fuelwood consumption by trekkers and local inhabitants. More than half a million dollars per year in tourism revenues have been earmarked for conservation, and large tracts of forests have been regenerated. WWF is also working with the governments of China, India, and Nepal to promote a trinational peace park at Kanchenjunga, which straddles all three nations.

The success of these and other initiatives depends on unprecedented human cooperation—between conservationists and farmers, local people and governments, and among nations, as many of the ecoregions extend across national boundaries. Since WWF first launched its Living Planet Campaign, heads of state and corporate leaders have risen to the challenge by making commitments to secure protection for nearly 1 billion acres of wildlife habitat in more than thirty countries—an area the size of the continental United States. But this is only a start. If we are truly to leave a living planet to those who follow us, then all of us must play a role. We must embrace the idea that our actions matter, that the decisions we make reverberate throughout the web of life and endure through time. In short, we must understand that all of us can make a difference.

To show what lies at stake, this book features images of some of the Global 200 ecoregions, photographed in vibrant color by three of the most talented photographers in the world. Serving as a clarion call to arms, their work stands as a testament to the legacy we stand to lose.

Frans Lanting, Galen Rowell, and David Doubilet are pioneers in the art of nature photography, each with a special style that sets him apart from the many others who make a living behind the lens. Frans Lanting offers us intimate portrayals of the lives of animals, revealing to us both their beauty and their mystery. Galen Rowell gained his reputation for his breathtaking mountain photography, bringing into our homes the stark beauty of the alpine world. And David Doubilet's photographs provide a window to the exotic world beneath the sea. Their images are presented here as a visual journey around the planet, illustrating the diversity of Global 200 ecoregions.

More than lensmen, they also care deeply about their subjects. "We're in an age of exploration under the sea," says David Doubilet, "the same kind of exploration that was happening on land in the late 1700s and early 1800s. But this time we know more about exploration, and what it can do to new worlds. I want people to appreciate and care enough about the world under the sea that they would be loath to harm it."

Galen Rowell emphasizes that throughout history people have gone to the natural world for spiritual refreshment. "It's not just a modern phenomenon, a way of getting away from cities. Jesus went into the wilderness to pray. Tibetans have always gone to the high country for pilgrimages. We need to preserve such places both for the sake of diversity and for the sake of all humanity."

"Galen, David, and I have had the opportunity to travel around the world multiple times covering a great variety of ecological subjects, and that has given us a unique perspective," says Frans Lanting. "We are able to see and compare places and show change over time. Many of the changes are disturbing, but I think our images help people become aware of what is happening beyond the horizon of their own lives."

The stunning images gracing these pages serve as visceral reminders of Earth's infinite variety. Biological diversity is our inheritance, a gift of this planet handed down through the ages. Will ours be the generation to see this treasure squandered forever? It lies within our power to leave our children a living planet.

"By presenting animals with their natural dignity and grace I offer them

FRANS LANTING

Growing up in a small village near Rotterdam, Frans Lanting found himself drawn to the slivers of wilderness that Holland has managed to retain.

"In Holland you learn to appreciate small niches of ecological diversity," he says. "As populated as it is, the country has kept many beaches, coastal dunes, and wetlands intact. That's where I spent my boyhood and that's where I began to observe animals and photograph nature."

His father was in business, an endeavor with little connection to the artistic pursuits that grew out of Frans's early naturalist experiences. As a child he learned to understand the differences between coastal dunes and inland dunes as well as varying water levels, and how they affected flora and fauna.

"I can't say why the natural world appealed to me, any more than a musician can say why he loves violins. I just heard the music in my head. I still do. To this day I feel happiest in a place with an endless horizon and the sight and the sounds of shorebirds all around."

The fate of that coastal habitat helped forge another facet of his future. The beloved dunes and wetlands near his village were eradicated and became the biggest petrochemical complex and industrial port in the world; bird songs were replaced by the bellows of ships' horns and the hisses of vented steam. These changes launched Frans's mission to use his photographic art in preserving segments of the natural world. "I think I can trace some of my roots as a conservationist to what happened there."

Still, family influences die hard. Although he continued to work at improving his photography, in 1977 he received a master's degree in environmental economics from Erasmus University in Rotterdam. A year later, in 1978, he embarked on a postgraduate program in environmental planning at the University of California at Santa Cruz. But a love of nature and interpreting it with photographs finally prevailed, and he left the academic world two years later to devote himself to photography. Now his life has become one of endless horizons and the

GALÁPAGOS ISLANDS, ECUADOR

Global 200 Ecoregion #126. A land iguana crosses a rocky beach under a brilliant sky (*left*). Despite the starkness left by volcanism, a profusion of unusual wildlife thrives here. One of two iguanas on the islands, this one burrows in the arid ground of the coastal areas while its marine relative swims in the sea.

Photographer: Frans Lanting

songs and scenes of the outdoors.

"It was a natural fit," he says, after publication of a dozen books and hundreds of articles in virtually every major magazine in the world including *National Geographic*, *GEO*, *Life*, *Audubon*, *Figaro*, and *Stern*. "My interest in wildlife goes beyond photography. I can be perfectly happy just watching animals without a camera.

"I like to make myself small and vulnerable around them. I believe you can open yourself up to animals by paying close attention to how they react to you. By becoming a passive element in their environment or through body language, I try to express my intentions, but I always will let the animals define the situation.

"I treat them as individuals. I've seen so many interesting things that defy standard textbook behavior. I've witnessed very subtle and complicated interactions among lions, albatrosses, even giant tortoises."

Early in his career, Frans began quietly observing animal communities. At one point he committed to a group of sanderlings that foraged along a beach on the central California coast, coming back to them for weeks. As they became accustomed to this deliberately moving human with his whirring, clicking camera, they let him get quite close, and he grew aware of not only their general behavior but also their idiosyncrasies.

"My photography of animals is preceded by lengthy observation," he says, "because unless I understand what is going on, my photos are just snapshots."

It's one thing to observe close-up the life of a diminutive shorebird and quite another to get under the skins of large predators or giants like elephants. In Africa, Frans followed a pride of lions for a month, becoming so much a noninterfering feature of their environment— almost an auxiliary lion—that one night they allowed him to photograph from a few feet away as they devoured a giraffe. Stretched out on his stomach near a water hole in the Kalahari Desert to photograph elephants, he was tested by the largest land mammal on Earth with bluff charges.

"It was a case of pushing my luck to the limit," he remembers. "I had spent several days by the water hole, until animals began to accept me as a fixture in the landscape. That wasn't too difficult with gazelles, but the elephants were another matter. One bull in particular would look at me and shake his head angrily or blow trunkfuls of water or dust my way. It became very important to sense whether he had things in mind that were too risky for me."

Such intimate encounters have resulted in memorable images that brought him international acclaim. In 1988 and 1989 he received top honors from World Press Photo for his work in Madagascar and the Antarctic. In 1991 the BBC named him Wildlife Photographer of the Year. Wilbur Garrett, editor of the *National Geographic Magazine* in the 1980s, referred to him as "the finest nature photographer working today." In 1997 he received the Ansel Adams award from the Sierra Club for his contributions to conservation through the art of photography. In the February 1999 issue of *National Geographic*, his photographs relating to biodiversity occupied two-thirds of the editorial pages, one of the largest presentations by one photographer in the magazine's 110-year history.

"Many people now have an appreciation for well-known large species like tigers or whales," Frans says. "But it's harder to get sympathy for complete ecosystems and all the smaller creatures that make up the foundation of much of the natural world. If we don't understand the

whole ecological fabric, the mega-mammals that we care so much about may not be around someday.

"Ultimately I do what I do because I love it. I really enjoy going out and spending time in nature, interacting with animals. But I also photograph with the conviction that my images can play a role in a public discourse about the future of our natural world."

Millions of people have learned to see faraway worlds through his eyes. His provocative coverage of Madagascar's unique flora and fauna and his graphic depiction of the ecological crisis unfolding on that island served as a call for action for scientists, conservationists, and funding agencies. Likewise, his seminal coverage of Botswana's Okavango Delta dramatically increased attention for what Frans believes is a place of global significance.

"I like to tell complex stories about how animals relate to landscapes. Even though an individual animal might look isolated in some of my compositions, I know that nothing could be further from the truth. They're all part of a continuity, and one that I hope people will realize includes us."

BORNEO

Global 200 Ecoregions #40, #41. Their reflection in the camera lens fascinates two orphaned orangutan youngsters (*above*), who are more than willing to cooperate with photographer Frans Lanting. Two other orphans cling together for mutual support at a rehabilitation center in northern Borneo (*left*), where they will gradually be reintroduced to the wild. Squeezed by shrinking habitats due to logging and agriculture, the orangutans number no more than 20,000 in Sumatra and Borneo.

Photographer: Frans Lanting

"If my life could be compared to a wheel, wilderness is the axle and

GALEN ROWELL

Nearing the age of thirty, Galen Rowell found himself in a dilemma. Wilderness outings at an early age with his parents had bred in him a love of the outdoors. He became an accomplished climber while still in his teens and found himself drawn to the bare-bones simplicity and raw beauty of high places. He also began developing skills in writing and photography.

But the times spent doing those things he loved were stolen hours. Despite a physics scholarship, no college field of study seemed able to combine what he did for sheer enjoyment with making a living. He began to document his climbs in Yosemite and the High Sierra and send articles to magazines. Nothing sold to the majors.

With no clear career goal in sight, he quit school and supported his wife, two young children, and himself with a small automotive service business near his home in Berkeley, California. "I thought I would have to settle for a life that had two parts—one in which I made a living and the other in which I enjoyed wild places," he says. The auto business was an interlude he thought might sustain him for a couple of years while he further explored what he wanted to do. It lasted ten.

In 1972, Galen followed his creative urges. He sold the business and turned his enjoyments into a freelance profession—writing, photographing, and lecturing about the alpine outdoors. "I had a little money from selling the business," he says, "but I came within fifty dollars of hitting rock bottom."

The break came within the first year when he agreed to help a photographer friend do a story on climbing in Yosemite for *National Geographic*. When the friend was called away on other work, the assignment went to Galen and the shoot became a cover story.

In the decades to come, Galen's adventures and photography would take him to the seven continents, both poles, and on more than twenty Himalayan expeditions. His climbing accomplishments include more than a hundred first ascents at the ends of the earth. His illustrated

CALIFORNIA, U.S.A.

Global 200 Ecoregion #75. Alpenglow beneath threatening storm clouds reflects in Evolution Lake along the John Muir Trail in Kings Canyon National Park *(left)*. The high alpine lake, named by a nineteenth century explorer and admirer of Charles Darwin, spills north and west to feed the San Joaquin River. At nearly 11,000 feet it often remains frozen into the midsummer.
Photographer: Galen Rowell

lectures, seminars, and photographic workshops have been attended by hundreds of thousands, and his fourteen books sell around the world. His love of the natural world and a desire to pass that on to others have finally come together.

"Physically I relate to the wilderness by climbing, skiing, hiking, and trail running," he says. "Visually I relate my love of the wilderness through photography, verbally through lectures, and by the written word through books and articles. Paying attention to my own survival on mountains has led me to see, with special clarity, the importance of global biodiversity in everything from old-growth forests to an evanescent tide pool."

At the heart of his memorable photographic style is the dedication to perceiving magical natural light and rendering it with integrity. Galen Rowell's photographs leap from a page with compelling color and form, a result of his careful study of the nature of light and what happens when it encounters film. No colored filters are used to achieve false hues. The viewer of his pictures realizes that such scenes could have been observed in his or her own experience.

Galen admits that his photographic career took a major leap when he realized a simple fact of physics: that all objects are colorless—black, that is—until they reflect or transmit light to which our brains assign colors. Thus, a critical part of good photography was not finding objects to record but the right light in which to record their myriad moods.

A major problem lies in understanding what the camera and film see, compared to what the human eye sees. To do that, Galen wrote a first-person narrative from the viewpoint of the film. It began:

"I am a frame of Kodachrome film waiting for you to open the shutter...We do not see color alike. The light-sensitive chemicals that trigger dyes during my development do not produce exactly the colors you see.

"If your companion is wearing a blue-and-red shirt, you think the shirt is the same color outside as it is indoors under artificial lighting. I know that isn't so. I record the same shirt in radically different colors in each situation..."

Humans, Galen realized, "create perceived colors in relation to one another no matter what the light source. Our ancestors needed to recognize the tawny coat of a Pleistocene lion by moonlight, dawn, or in the noonday sun. But film, with no brain and no lions to worry about, has a fixed color response to wavelength. It also can't ignore shadows or correct perspective the way our brain simplifies our retinal image."

Galen calls the chasm between what his eyes see

and what his film records "the visionary wilderness." He has been exploring it for over thirty years, learning that the same effects that at first caused most of his nature photos not to "come out" could be used creatively to give an image added visual power. Understanding these differences may not lead him to a single answer to that eternal question about the meaning of life, but it has provided him with multiple visual responses that answer a more pertinent question for him: What life experiences are the most worth living?

To share his world with others, Galen is constantly visiting high and wild places, usually with his wife and business partner, Barbara, who manages their Emeryville gallery and office called Mountain Light. He believes there is a strong similarity between what people in Asia call a pilgrimage and what people in the United States call a wilderness adventure. Both involve experiencing hardship in the wilds for a spiritual reward. "Though now I sometimes go into the wilderness to earn a living, most of the things I choose to do because I want to do them for their own sake."

During the course of producing a book, Galen recently revisited places in the San Francisco Bay Area that he had explored as a youth. "I began to see these wild places near home in a whole new light. Earlier, when I really wanted to be climbing in Yosemite or traveling to exotic places around the world, those wild places in the Bay Area seemed like wilderness with training wheels. Now, having been to natural wonders on all seven continents, it is clear to me that my Bay Area photographs hold their own against the natural splendor of more exotic places."

Bay Area Wild became a 1997 regional best-seller, emphasizing the importance of the remaining fragments of the natural world that exist amidst urban areas. It also led to his participation in this book.

"My goal was first to say, 'Hey, look what we have here.' That leads to looking farther around and saying, 'Hey, look, it's not just the natural superlatives that are worth saving, it's also what's in our own backyards.'

"The Dalai Lama told me that you don't have to be in a spectacular place to gain spiritual inspiration. The more enlightened your being, the less you need to awaken that spiritual side. His philosophy is also based on the concept of universal responsibility embracing all mankind as well as nature. For me, that's the central message of this book and why I feel so privileged to be a part of it."

CALIFORNIA, U.S.A.

Global 200 Ecoregion #75. The marriage of mountaineering and photography has resulted in thousands of memorable images, including this one at Horsetail Fall *(left)* on the one day of the year when last light comes at sunset. Photographer Galen Rowell's long climbing career includes hundreds of first ascents, and precarious perches such as this foot- and handhold *(above)* alongside Yosemite Falls.

Photographer: Galen Rowell

"I want to sweep aside the dark gauze that covers the sea and show
people a world that is barely imaginable to them."

DAVID DOUBILET

From unlikely arenas—the streets of New York and the shores of New Jersey—sprang a brilliant career in underwater photography. David Doubilet combined a love of color and a passion for diving to record an amazing world beneath the waves.

"I grew up seeing the work of Jacques Cousteau and the first *National Geographic* underwater still photographer, Luis Marden," says David, "and from an early age I knew exactly what I wanted to do in life. By the time I was nine or ten I was snorkeling in the ocean near my parents' summer home in Elberon, New Jersey. I also liked art and spent a lot of time in art museums in the city, so color was always important to me."

At the age of twelve he became S.C.U.B.A. certified at the 92nd Street YMCA pool. In the long summer days he would snorkel and spear fish off the jetties of Elberon that extend into the Atlantic ocean like dark teeth. "On a good day the visibility was about ten feet, but the desire to make pictures soon overcame the hunting craziness.

"My first underwater camera was a Brownie Hawkeye. My father was a doctor, and he brought an anesthesiologist's rubber bag home from the hospital. I put the camera in the bag and taped the opening to a face mask that let me manipulate the controls through the bag and shoot out the front of the mask. The pictures were awful!"

But he was hooked. His father, hoping young David would head for a career in medicine or science, spoke to his English teacher, Gus Trowbridge, with concern, "All the kid wants to do is swim underwater and take pictures."

"So, let him," replied the teacher. Resigned, Dr. Henry Doubilet took his young son to Andros Island in the Bahamas the next summer for his first dives in waters with real clarity. A dive resort owner, Dick Birch, seeing his enthusiasm, gave him a summer job and the opportunity for more diving. At fifteen he was a divemaster, leading tourists underwater off the Bahamas.

Graduating from the Brownie and the rubber bag to actual marine cameras, he began winning contests in

CAYMAN ISLANDS, CARIBBEAN SEA

Global 200 Ecoregion #199. Sea and sky blend as stingrays forage through shallow water in North Sound, Grand Cayman Island *(left).* Fishermen cleaning their catch nearby and throwing scraps into the sea often draw the flat, mysterious fish. When two divers joined them in the water in the 1980s, the rays disproved a reputation for viciousness by docilely eating from their hands.

Photographer: David Doubilet

underwater photography. He sold his first picture before he had a driver's license, and his work was displayed at a film festival featuring underwater photography at the Massachusetts Institute of Technology. There he met *National Geographic* diver and photographer Bates Littlehales, who encouraged him to show a portfolio to Robert Gilka, the legendary director of photography at the *National Geographic* magazine.

"Gilka looked at my pictures for about two minutes and, in that gruff manner of his, pronounced there was 'nothing new' in them. Bates suggested that I was limited by the equipment I was using, so I bought better cameras."

Undeterred by the review of his work, David paid his own way to Israel, where *National Geographic* was shooting a story on marine biologist Eugenie Clark's study of garden eels. He produced several outstanding photographs that were published in the article, in which he shared the photographic byline. Since "The Red Sea's Gardens of Eels" appeared in November of 1972, nearly fifty articles with Doubilet pictures have appeared in the *National Geographic*. Assignments have taken him to waters around the world. Among many awards, he won first place in the National Press Photographers' Association (NPPA) in the science/natural history category for his work in New Zealand waters and has received several honorable mentions by NPPA over the past decade.

Although most of his photographic work has been for *National Geographic*, David's photographs and writing have also appeared worldwide in other magazines and books. His wife, Anne, who wrote the text for the book *Under the Sea from A to Z*, and their teenage daughter, Emily, also dive.

David's sea creatures startle viewers with their brilliance. Words don't always suffice when he tries to explain how it comes about: "It's color, it's composition, it's lighting. It's the help I get from friends who live in the area where I'm shooting and know it well. It's what I feel about the subject itself. I'm lucky to have had a classical visual education. So I'm thinking a lot about color and art when I'm swimming around under the sea."

The photographic lighting expert Harold "Doc" Edgerton, who took the young diver under his wing, "gave me sunlight to put under the sea," David would say later. He also admits that looking over directors' shoulders while shooting stills for the feature films *The Deep* and *Splash* taught him movie lighting techniques to illuminate fish.

His work is not without its risks. A moray eel mistook his hand for a squid and bit clean through it with razor sharp teeth. "It felt like an electric shock," he says, then adds with typical laconic humor, "It also gave me a good excuse to decline when people asked me to play the banjo." He's become, for obvious reasons, a student of shark behavior. "You can push them and push yourself, and then you learn by their movements when it's time to clear out."

The hardest thing to accomplish in underwater photography, he says, is communicating what you feel beyond simply showing the subject itself. He cites a memorable photograph that shows a stingray gliding under the water while puffy cumulus clouds float above the surface on a brilliant day.

"You have this primitive, weird creature that looks like an airplane, and the clouds overhead, but the subliminal message you are trying to convey is the incredible clarity of the water, which is one of the great gifts of the Earth."

Lack of clarity, both in Earthly waters and human vision, has troubled him through the years. "Underwater photography was just coming of age when I was fourteen or fifteen years old," he says. "At that time, all the talk was of conquering this new frontier, how we might live under the sea some day. Now there's more of an awareness of what is happening to the oceans.

"At the age of sixteen I got a job diving for Sandy Hook Marine Lab, twelve miles from New York Harbor, where they were dumping lead and zinc and who knows what else. We began to see what was happening in the food chain and to populations of bluefish, silversides, and menhaden.

"I knew about pollution problems early on. The bigger problem is overfishing. If someone had told you ten or fifteen years ago that the Grand Banks, that great refrigerator of fish in the Atlantic Ocean, would be closed, you would have said they were crazy. All you have to do to grasp the problem is go to the fish markets of Tokyo to see how much we are consuming.

"I think it's important to show a side of the planet that most people never see, so they'll care more about it. I want them to know about mountain ranges greater than anything on land, canyons deeper than anything we can stand beside. I want them to realize that the sea's flowers are animals, more colorful than any garden. I've taken pictures of things underwater that are so incredible that as I'm looking through the viewfinder I'm shaking my head with disbelief. How could anything be so beautiful? There are extraordinary shapes, brilliant colors, amazing adaptations.

"But these are recent discoveries. Up until the last fifty years we've only been looking at the ocean like an undulating skin, not seeing the wildlife and the landscapes underneath it. We've got to learn more about it and take care of it or it will be gone. After all, humans came from the sea. It's the cauldron of life and we know very little about the life that is there.

"It's not a skin, it's a doorway. Once you realize that, you can never look at the sea in the same way again."

FLORIDA KEYS, U.S.A.

Global 200 Ecoregion #199. Loggerhead turtles *(left)* mate on the sea floor in Key Largo National Marine Sanctuary, the male clinging to the female's shell with tiny claws at the ends of his flippers. Inches away Mauricio Handler photographs Doubilet recording the scene with camera and strobe light *(above)*.

Photographer: David Doubilet

GALÁPAGOS ISLANDS, ECUADOR: *Global 200 Ecoregion #230.* Eating piecemeal, a juvenile sea lion grabs black-tipped salema one at a time after cornering them at the edge of an underwater shelf off the Galápagos Islands. When the 1997–98 El Niño depleted its usual fare of squid and lantern fish, the sea lion turned to these small fish, normally not worth the energy depleted in catching them. The Galápagos, a scattering of volcanic protrusions 600 miles west of South America, have become a symbol of biological diversity because of the unique life-forms that developed here, inspiring Charles Darwin to formulate his theories of evolution. Today, these flagships of speciation have also become symbols of humankind's ability to upset the balance of fragile ecosystems by careless encroachment. *Photographer: David Doubilet*

"The Earth does not belong to man; man belong

All things are connected like the blood which un

GALÁPAGOS ISLANDS, ECUADOR

Global 200 Ecoregion #126. Volcanoes that gave birth to the Galápagos left craters like footprints on Isabela Island *(left)*.
Seawater has partially filled two dormant cavities, although volcanism remains active elsewhere on the island. In the background
rises a huge volcano shaped like a warrior's shield by very fluid lava that oozes from inner Earth rather than erupting violently.
Part of the unique collection of species on the islands, marine iguanas up to six feet long are the world's only sea-going lizards *(above)*.
Diving underwater they eat seaweed and gnaw lichens from submerged boulders. On a higher, cooler part of Isabela where
mists nurture grasses and shrubs, a giant tortoise yawns *(following pages)*. Predation by humans and by the species they introduced
have depleted the numbers of tortoises from perhaps 250,000 to fewer than 20,000. The Spanish name for tortoise—*galápagos*—gave
the islands their name. Weighing up to 600 pounds, the tortoises served as long-term provisions for sailors of the seventeenth
to nineteenth centuries, who found the tortoises could survive in the holds of ships up to a year without food.

Photographer: Frans Lanting

GALÁPAGOS ISLANDS, ECUADOR

Global 200 Ecoregion #126. A variety of ecoregions in these islands is created by a climate modified by
the Humboldt Current out of Antarctica. A dry forest of palo santo trees climbs the slope of a volcano on Isabela Island (*left*),
touched by frequent mists and infrequent rains, while cacti crowd a drier area in the lowlands (*above*). Goats, dogs, cats,
and rats introduced by sailors and settlers make the lives of native species on the arid islands even more precarious by predation
and competition with them for food. A permanent population of some 14,000 people lives in the Galápagos. Overfishing
and illegal fishing offshore threaten the profusion of life that exists above the surface and depends on ocean resources for survival.
Still, scientists and tourists alike celebrate the islands for their diversity of fascinating life-forms.

Photographer: Frans Lanting

GALÁPAGOS ISLANDS, ECUADOR

Global 200 Ecoregion #230. Headed for a cooling bath and perhaps an underwater snack, a marine iguana *(left)* leaves the rocks
of Hood Island as two others consider following. Regulating body temperature requires the cold-blooded lizards to alternate between
the cold sea and the black, basaltic rocks that absorb heat in the tropical sun. As blue as the sea are the feet of the blue-footed
booby *(above)*. The pelagic bird frequents the islands as well as the mainland of South America. Among the multitudes of birds
are thirteen species of finches with varied bill shapes and feeding habits that evolved from a common ancestor.
Noting such adaptations during his visit in 1835 helped Charles Darwin shape his theory of evolution.
Photographer: Galen Rowell

GALÁPAGOS ISLANDS, ECUADOR: *Global 200 Ecoregion #230.* At ease with another sunbather *(above)*, a sea lion makes itself comfortable on the leg of a naturalist guide for visitors to the islands. After lacking natural enemies on land over the millennia, wildlife in the Galápagos shows almost no fear of humans. In a successful effort to protect such innocents and help maintain the ecosystem, the government of Ecuador now requires that tourists to Galápagos parklands be accompanied by a certified guide. Most of the islands' 3,000 square miles were declared a national park in 1959, the centennial of the publication of *The Origin of Species*. Another inhabitant of these teeming islands, a great frigate bird *(top, right)* puffs out his red gular sacs to entice females to his corner of real estate. A Sally Lightfoot crab puts its best feet forward on lava thousands of years old that looks as if it just cooled yesterday *(right)*. *Photographer: Galen Rowell*

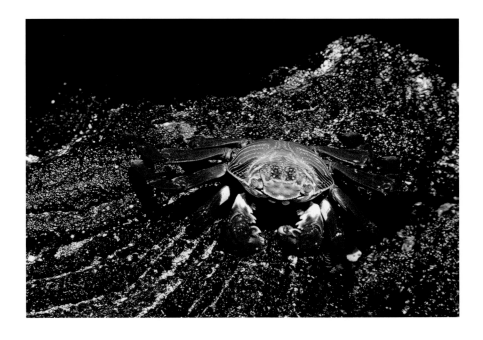

NORTHERN PERU

Global 200 Ecoregion #12. A shower-washed rain forest in the lowlands *(preceding pages)* along the Tambopata River
displays the botanical variety that makes this ecosystem so rich in species. At the foot of the Andes sprawl some 50,000 square
miles that were spared the development of neighboring areas. Brightening a river bank with their brilliant colors, macaws
feed on clay *(left)*. Scientists puzzle over the practice, suspecting the birds need the soil for minerals they lack, or to offset toxicity
of certain seeds they eat. Their diet and that of smaller parrots includes the bright blossoms of the flowering erythrina tree *(above)*.
Collection for the pet business threatened the macaws, largest of the parrots, until an international treaty outlawed the trade.
Native groups have long hunted the three-foot birds for food along the Tambopata. Peru has now designated the region
a national park and is attempting to enlist the hunters as guides for ecotourists.
Photographer: Frans Lanting

CORDILLERA BLANCA, PERU

Global 200 Ecoregion #106. In the higher, more arid habitat of the Andes, a family herds its
alpacas past a *puya raymondi (above)*, largest of the world's bromeliads—plants that acquire most of their food
and moisture from the air instead of the ground. The water-storing *puya* can stretch to 30–40 feet and
is found around 10,000 feet in the Andes. A giant hummingbird *(right)*, larger than a sparrow and a colossus
among its kind, nearly disappears against the barbed plant as it seeks nectar from the flowers.
Photographer: Galen Rowell

PATAGONIA, SOUTH AMERICA

The wind is your constant companion in Patagonia, where legendary gales of the latitudes known as the Furious Fifties blast unfettered onto the tip of South America. Wind shapes everything—the bizarre curves of rock, the contortions of tree trunks, your attitude after a day of leaning into its icy knife.

Here mountains erupt from the surface in a way seldom seen. Fitz Roy, named for the captain of the *Beagle* that brought naturalist Charles Darwin here in 1834, rears to 11,073 feet out of an arid plain. I awoke one morning fifty miles away to see its sculpted tower bathed in the crimson light of dawn, a vision of Oz.

Bizarre wildlife add to the other-world quality of this strange land. Guanacos, ancestors of the llama, seem to float through the thorny bushes, their long necks held gracefully in the air. Ostrichlike rheas bound about on long legs while giant condors circle overhead.

Neither nation nor state, Patagonia is the geographic region straddling Argentina and Chile, where the continent

---

PATAGONIA, CHILE: *Global 200 Ecoregion #100.* Guanacos (*left*), wild relatives of llamas and camels, browse before the Torres del Paine in the national park named for the granite towers. The sure-footed beasts run nimbly over land that has been made rugged by tectonic uplift, glaciers, and hurricane-force winds. The one adult male in a group of half a dozen females drives off the young when they are a year old, forcing males to join a bachelor herd and females to attach to another group. *Photographer: Galen Rowell*

PATAGONIA, CHILE: *Global 200 Ecoregion #100*. Sunrise touches the Cuernos del Paine *(below)*, where suspended glacial silt paints Lake Pehoe a vivid turquoise. Glaciers flowing from a massive ice cap carved the horn-shaped peaks during eons of slow journeys down valleys of granite. Soaring among the peaks is an Andean condor *(right)* in the prime of its life. The 25-pound carrion-eaters depend on thermal currents for flying, and flap their wings only rarely between takeoffs and landings. *Photographer: Galen Rowell*

ends in a rage of wind, ice, and rock. Its jagged monoliths and strange creatures stand out from land laid bare by the wind, a domain of huge sheep ranches, and national parks. Don't look for any Club Meds or golf courses. Patagonia holds the reputation of having some of the world's worst weather.

Climbing icy Fitz Roy my partners and I retreated several times in the face of winds that must have reached 150 miles per hour and blew some of our carefully stashed equipment into oblivion. But the view from the top at dawn will be forever etched in my mind. To the west, more than two hundred miles of continental glaciers stretched to the horizon. To the east, the vast, treeless pampa was limitless. Not far below us were the jagged spires of Cerro Torre and a great lake named Viedma, fed by an arm of glacier that calves icebergs in its waters.

The land challenges its visitors, but as wild places shrink in number, ever more people are coming to absorb Patagonia's unique scenery. I'm grateful for my many visits to experience its raw beauty.

PATAGONIA, CHILE

Global 200 Ecoregion #100. Fire and ice seem to blend as sunrise strikes Cerro Torre and its
satellite spires *(left)*, while behind it stretches the blue of the 200-mile-long Great Patagonian Ice Cap.
Sunrise below Fitz Roy *(above)* highlights two effects of Patagonia's notorious high winds—
a flagged southern beech tree and lenticular clouds that signify an approaching storm.
Photographer: Galen Rowell

"A man in the woods comes face to face with the creation, of which he must begin to see himself a part."

—WENDELL BERRY

PATAGONIA, CHILE

Global 200 Ecoregion #77. Relatives of cedars and redwoods, endangered alerce trees *(left)* can live well beyond 3,000 years, if they avoid being felled for lumber. Once more common, the huge trees now survive only in remote forests. Another species of ancient origins, the arucaria *(top)*, or "monkey puzzle" tree, on the slopes of the Villarica volcano is the progenitor of all pines. Often barren and rugged, Patagonia merges here into temperate rain forest in southern Chile. A river flows through Pumalin Natural Park *(above)*, 1,500 square miles of temperate rain forest gifted to Chile in 1997 by environmental activist Doug Tompkins. He purchased a vast tract of forest from Reñihue Fjord on the ocean to the Argentine border, to save it from logging.

Photographer: Galen Rowell

AN ESSAY BY FRANS LANTING

PANTANAL, BRAZIL

Dense, steamy jungle lines both sides of the river as I drift with the quiet current. Then my boat rounds a bend and the vegetation opens to a rookery of wading birds that erupts in raucous commotion. Grinning caimans lie on the sandy banks, waiting for a hapless chick to topple from a nest. A few yards further and the forest opens into a broad savanna dotted with grazing capybara, the world's largest rodent.

Brazil's little-known Pantanal enchants me with its variety of landscapes, host to many species that are disappearing elsewhere. Here giant otters frolic in the water and the jaguar still rules the night. Endangered hyacinth macaws wing over the forest and swamp in rare profusion. Below them lurks the highest concentration of crocodilians anywhere.

This largest wetland in the world pulses like a giant heart in the center of South America. Half the year heavy rains spread a sheet of water that pumps nutrients into a basin larger than Uruguay. The Pantanal acts like a sponge, retaining water and holding back downstream floods. Anteaters, jaguars, armadillos, and flightless rheas retreat to islands of solid ground. Fish leave the rivers to feed in flooded pastures and in turn feed thousands

---

PANTANAL, BRAZIL: *Global 200 Ecoregion #103.* In the center of South America, water appears plentiful on the Paraguay River but smoke fills the air from agricultural fires on parched lands nearby *(left).* Half the year rains flood the flat grasslands, nurturing wildlife that has adjusted to the wet-dry rhythms. *Photographer: Frans Lanting*

of wading storks, egrets, and herons. Migrating birds from as far away as Canada join Brazilian ducks in immense flocks.

When the rains stop, streams recede to their channels and water relieved of sediment seeps slowly from the Pantanal Basin. Rank grasses emerge in the open savanna, providing grazing for wildlife. Waders and swimmers gather at isolated pools.

It's important not to disturb these annual rhythms. Due to conservation efforts made by farmers and ranchers and cutbacks in poaching, ocelots and jaguars, once nearly depleted, are bouncing back. Most important, more Brazilians now care about preserving the Pantanal, so this is a story with hope. Perhaps the caiman has a reason to smile.

PANTANAL, BRAZIL: *Global 200 Ecoregion #103.* When the rains cease and floods shrink, waters retreat to isolated pools *(left).* The distribution of fish from riverbeds into the surrounding lands makes them more accessible to wading birds such as the great egret *(below),* here in spring breeding plumage. The annual movement of water through the Pantanal makes it a destination for water-birds in Brazil and migratory birds from as far away as North America. *Photographer: Frans Lanting*

PANTANAL, BRAZIL

Global 200 Ecoregion #103. A collared anteater *(left),* the smaller of two in the Pantanal, rears in defensive posture.

Though it stands only two feet high, the long claws that rip open anthills can inflict serious damage on an attacker. Both anteater

species lick up ants and termites with long, sticky tongues. Largest rodent in the world, the capybara *(above)* can weigh 100 pounds.

Semiaquatic, it grazes on riverside grass but when danger approaches flees to water, where its webbed feet make it an adept swimmer.

It can stay submerged for several minutes. Another denizen of wetlands and rivers, a caiman emerges from a lagoon *(following pages).*

Poachers for the skin trade seriously depleted the caiman population until regulations curbed hunting. On the comeback,

Pantanal caimans now number some 10 million, the highest concentration in the world.

Photographer: Frans Lanting

PANTANAL, BRAZIL

Global 200 Ecoregion #103. As waters recede from surrounding lands in the dry season, wading birds, including egrets and wood storks, congregate at small pools *(above)* to harvest small fish and amphibians stranded there. Water lily pads a yard wide line the banks along the Paraguay River *(right).* Some grow large enough to support a small child.

Photographer: Frans Lanting

ATLANTIC FOREST, BRAZIL

Global 200 Ecoregion #13. In contrast to the flat interior, Brazil's Atlantic Forest *(preceding pages)* varies in altitude from 650 to 5,000 feet, creating numerous ecozones that support millions of species. Lords of the trees, muriquis, or woolly spider monkeys *(left)*, frolic in the Atlantic Forest. These largest of the New World monkeys live in a shrinking habitat. Only 5 percent of the dense forests that existed when the first European colonists arrived here in the early sixteenth century now remain. The rest have been leveled for agriculture and development. A smaller forest dweller, the golden lion tamarin *(above)* has been reduced to perhaps 1,000 individuals by poaching for the fur and pet trades. At one time, more tamarins existed in captivity than in the wild, sparking a consortium of zoos and conservation groups to breed and reintroduce the rare marmosets into the forest.

Photographer: Frans Lanting

IGUAÇÚ, BRAZIL: *Global 200 Ecoregion #13.* The thunder of plummeting water can be heard for miles around Iguaçú Falls *(right)*, the most immense waterfalls in the world. Over a space of some two and a half miles, more than twenty cataracts pour over cliffs an average of 200 feet high, separated by masses of rocks and tree-covered islands. The falls highlight the nearly 800-square-mile Iguaçú National Park, one of the largest remaining portions of Brazil's Atlantic Forest and home to species such as the green-billed toucan *(above)*. Close-up views in the dense vegetation *(following pages)* reveal more uniqueness at risk: a strangely striated plant that creates a leaf within a leaf, and one of the many orchids that decorates the forest. *Photographer: Frans Lanting*

COASTAL BELIZE: *Global 200 Ecoregion #197*. In Central America, mangrove islets *(preceding pages)* dot the warm Caribbean Sea where water and sky seem to meld. *Photographer: Frans Lanting*

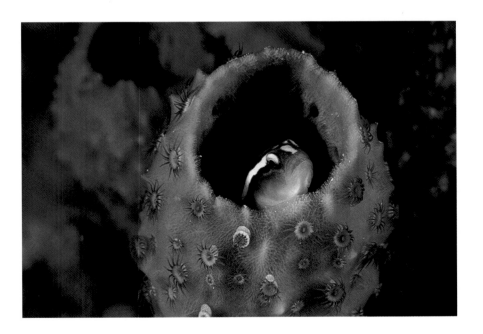

COASTAL BELIZE: *Global 200 Ecoregion #197*. Beneath the surface, filter-feeding tunicates blossom on the arm of a sponge *(left)* to harvest drifting nutrients. In the larval stage they anchor themselves on the larger host. Stony corals *(top)* open to comb plankton from the water while a blue-striped goby swims across a host of open mouths. In exchange for camou-flaged shelter, the small fish cleans out detritus that settles between the polyps. In deeper seclusion, a yellow-striped goby peeks from its hiding place inside a tube sponge *(above)*. *Photographer: David Doubilet*

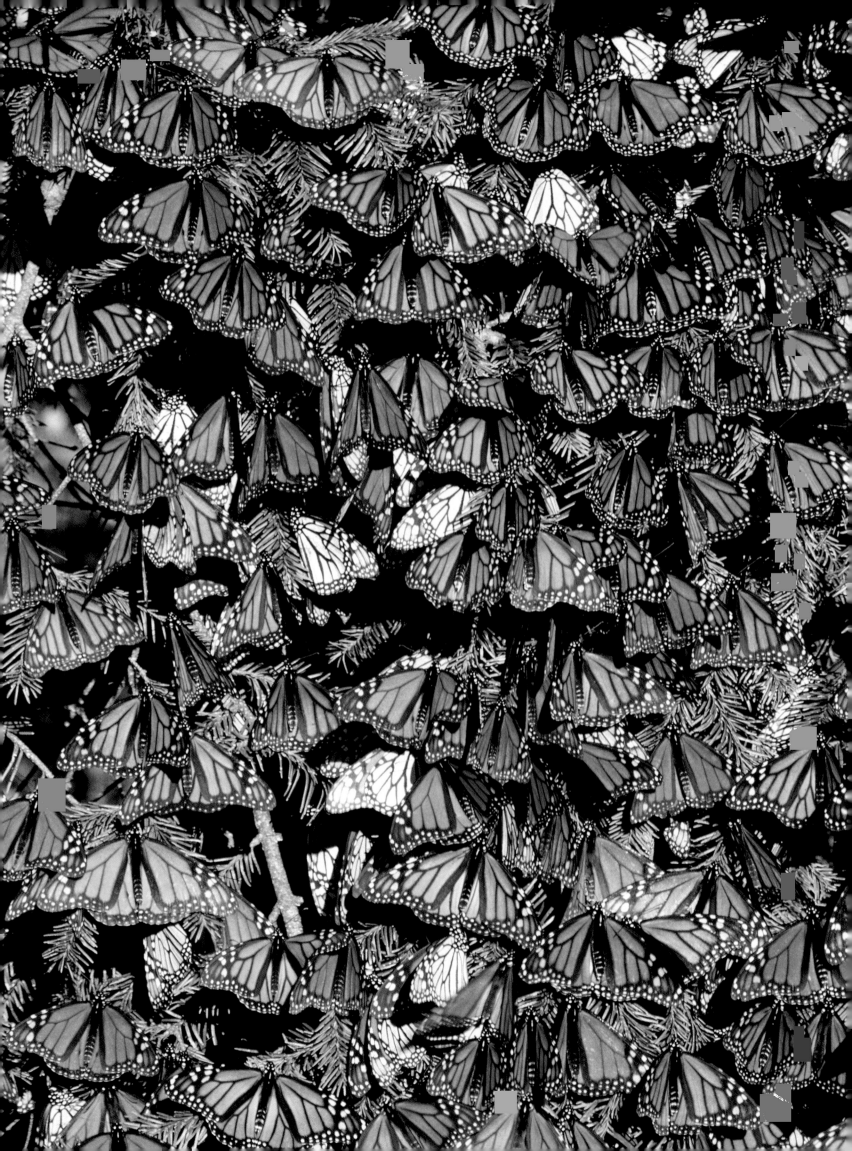

MICHOACÁN, MEXICO

Global 200 Ecoregion #83. Tapestries of monarch butterflies drape oyamel trees at 7,000–9,000 feet (*left*)
to escape the cold of the North American winter. Their weight sometimes breaks branches.
Every autumn, millions journey thousands of miles from the eastern U.S. and Canada to the highlands of central
Mexico, where they perch in semidormancy (*above*) before the spring warmth sends them back north.
Photographer: Frans Lanting

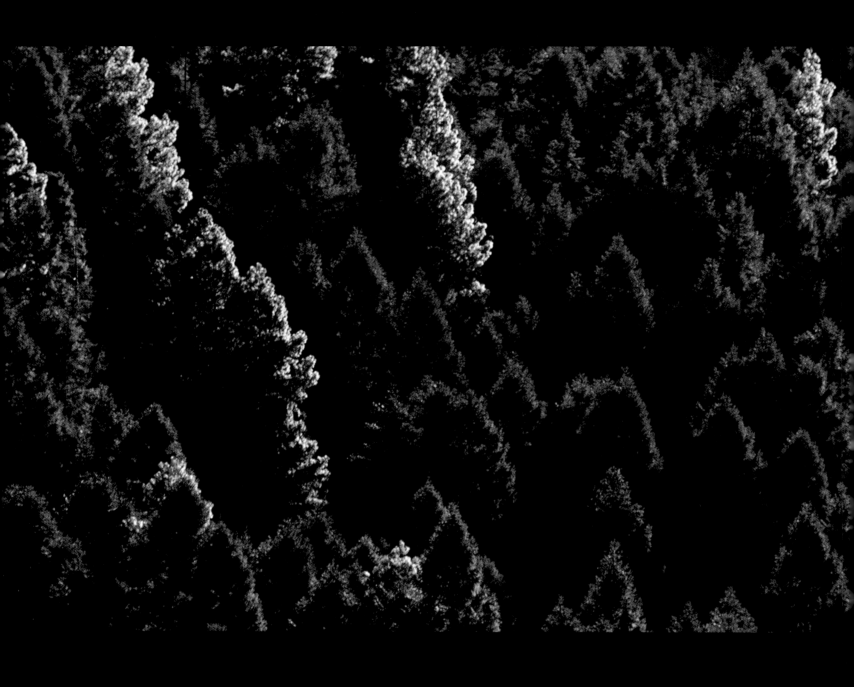

SIERRA MADRE ORIENTAL, MEXICO

Global 200 Ecoregions #83, #124. Gaps made by woodcutters in a pine and fir forest *(left)*
could affect the population of monarch butterflies. Hordes of the orange and black voyagers, familiar
to North Americans, winter in the high forests and survive best under an intact canopy. In the arid
lowlands, an agave plant spreads its thick leaves amid a tangle of jojoba *(above)*.
Photographer: Frans Lanting

BAJA, MEXICO

Global 200 Ecoregion #124. Barren sand dunes of the Baja peninsula *(left)* stretch along
the shores of important breeding grounds for gray whales. The leviathans migrate from the Bering Sea
to a few well-protected lagoons such as Magdalena Bay, visible at upper right, to mate and calve.
Photographer: Galen Rowell

EVERGLADES, FLORIDA, U.S.A.

Global 200 Ecoregions #102, #84. Across the continent from the Baja, the Everglades offer a rich breeding ground
for smaller aquatic creatures and numerous birds. Twilight reflects in Pine Glades Lake in Everglades National Park,
part of the flat terrain where a sheet of water slowly works its way to the sea over the Florida peninsula *(above).*
Bedrock under this lake keeps it flooded year-round, while the sawgrass prairies that dominate the Everglades alternately
flood and emerge. On solid ground at Lone Pine Key *(following pages),* sunrise on a misty morning appears to
set ablaze the conifers and lush vegetation beneath them.
Photographer: Galen Rowell

"They are, they always have been, one of the unique regions of the Earth, remote, never wholly known."

—MARJORIE STONEMAN DOUGLAS

EVERGLADES, FLORIDA, U.S.A.

Global 200 Ecoregion #102. Displaying the long neck that gives it the nickname "snakebird,"
an anhinga *(left)* dries its feathers in the sun. Commonly seen in the Everglades, the bird opens its plumage in
water to lose buoyancy and aid in its submarine pursuit of fish. Few trees but dwarf cypress *(top)* can grow in
the sodden soils of the park, in an area known as Pa-hay-okee. Life looks precarious for a red-bellied turtle *(above)*
as an alligator approaches, but the swamp's top predator passed by harmlessly.
Photographer: Galen Rowell99

EVERGLADES, FLORIDA, U.S.A.

Global 200 Ecoregion #102. The long-stemmed head of a tricolored heron *(left)* stretches out of sawgrass prairie,
the basic habitat of the Everglades. In the rainy season, the grass nearly disappears under moving water. The Everglades
supports some of the highest biodiversity in North America, but agricultural runoff and diversion of water for urban
use threaten the "river of grass." Federal and state programs now attempt to restore the habitat to its natural condition.
A highly endangered Florida panther *(above)*, a secretive creature requiring plenty of cover, peers from hiding.
Photographer: Galen Rowell

CARIBBEAN SEA

This is a friendly sea with a subtle palette of color, a Monet rather than a Jackson Pollock. I did my first real diving in the Caribbean, and returning to its warm embrace is like coming back to an old friend.

A swim along a reef in many tropical seas is like a walk through a jungle, but in the Caribbean it is a stroll through a simple, lovely garden. It is a small sea physically contained on the west—it's kept by the Isthmus of Panama from touching the rest of the world's warm oceans—and bordered to the east by the North and South Atlantic.

It's also a gentle, welcoming world, with intense beauty and water often clear as glass. When you compare the Caribbean to other warm seas, it is similar to comparing the great plains of North America to the savannas of Africa—it is a place much more amenable to humans. Just as the great plains have grasslands but no lions, the Caribbean has reefs with no sea snakes and shores with no saltwater crocodiles.

FLORIDA KEYS, U.S.A.: *Global 200 Ecoregions #102, #199.* Slow-flowing waters of the Everglades eventually reach Florida Bay and the northern waters of the Caribbean Sea *(left)*. Here small islands of mangrove lie scattered over thousands of square miles between the Florida Keys and the tip of mainland Florida, an area known as the "back country." Shallows two to ten feet deep serve as a protective nursery for many fish, a mating area for groupers, and a feeding ground for tarpon and bonefish. Development along the Florida coast threatens marine life with pollution. *Photographer: David Doubilet*

As warm seas go, it is far above the equator, and
that has contributed to a rather exclusive list of inhabitants. The last great ice age chilled the waters of the
Caribbean and caused many species to die out. Unlike
other reef areas, it was too isolated for the lost members
to be replaced by a huge variety of species that evolved
in warm-water basins elsewhere. There are nearly 80
types of corals compared with more than 400 in other
parts of the world, perhaps 750 species of fish compared
with 3,000–4,000 in the Indo-Pacific. It does have,
however, the most complete collection of sponges.

Being enclosed makes it much more fragile and
requires our mindful care even more. We have already
wiped out the lobsters and jewfish in its western waters.
We should not expect the Caribbean to feed the many
people that live along its shores, but its gentle beauty
can long nurture our appreciation of a friendly sea.

FLORIDA KEYS, U.S.A.: *Global 200 Ecoregion #199.* Blue-striped grunts *(left)* cluster for protection in the shade of a shipwreck off Key Largo. Partnering in the deep, a gray angelfish allows a bite-size neon goby to clean its mouth and gills with impunity *(below)*. A male sea horse *(below, left)* shows a belly distended with its young as it moves toward a perch that it will grasp with its long tail. Live babies born to the female swim through an opening into the male's abdomen to brood before emerging in a second rebirth. *Photographer: David Doubilet*

CAYMAN ISLANDS, CARIBBEAN SEA: *Global 200 Ecoregion #199.* A blizzard of bait fish nearly obscures a diver swimming near the mouth of an underwater cave *(above)*. Sometimes called silversides, bait fish bloom in enormous numbers only to become prey for larger neighbors. Also seen from below, needlefish *(above, right)* blending with flashes of surface light demonstrate their excellent camouflage. Made ghostlike by its coloration, a file fish *(right)* looks transparent against a sea fan. The dark color of a young Atlantic spotted dolphin *(following pages)* will resemble that of its mother when it grows to adulthood. By day, the two socialize with others in shallows off the Grand Bahama Bank, rooting out razor fish in the sand. At night they enter deep water to feed on squid. *Photographer: David Doubilet*

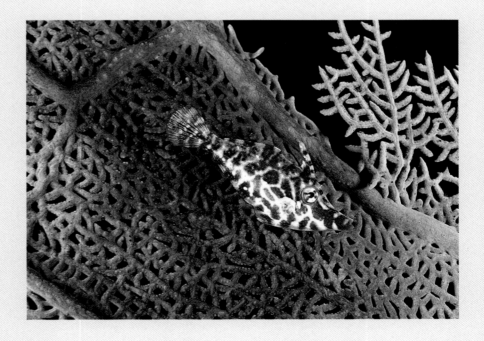

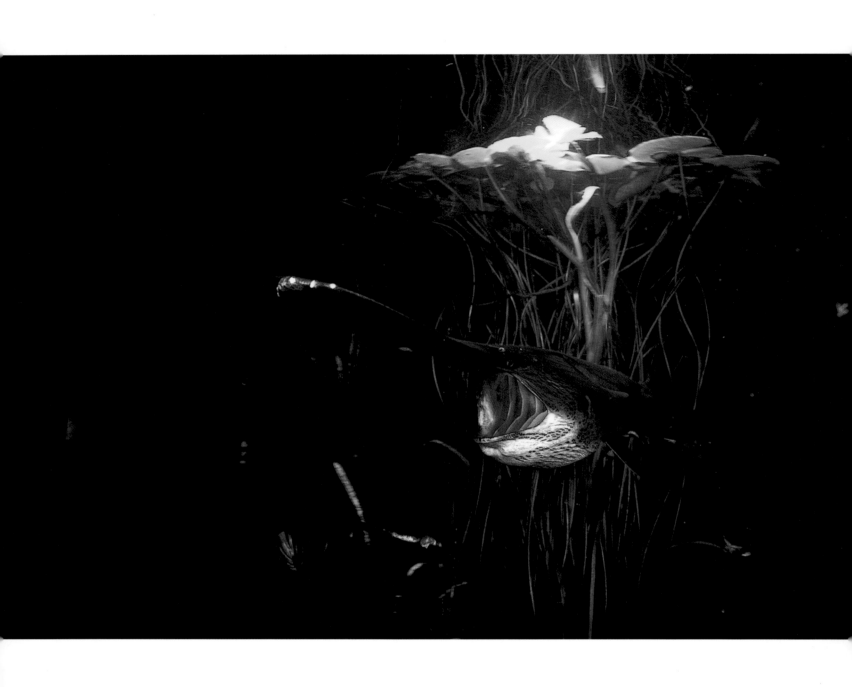

EASTERN UNITED STATES

Global 200 Ecoregions #139, #218. With the look of a river monster, a paddlefish *(left)* in the Tennessee River
opens its mouth wide to take in water and plankton. Like many whales, it has a filtering system that retains food as water flows
out the gills. The paddlelike protuberance steadies the fish while it cruises and feeds. Some paddlefish grow to 300 pounds.
Another strange river creature, a lake sturgeon *(above)* with plates and scutes like a crocodile, hovers in the St. Lawrence River
between the U.S. and Canada. A bottom-feeder, it feeds on crustaceans and invertebrates including the exotic zebra mussels
currently invading North American waters. Most of the twenty-six species of sturgeon in the world are highly endangered due
to overfishing for the caviar trade and dam-building, which changes river dynamics.
Photographer: David Doubilet

EASTERN UNITED STATES

Global 200 Ecoregions #139, #64. Fall brushes color onto foliage around a stream in the highlands area of
North Carolina *(left).* Oaks and maples turn red and gold as fall days shorten in the Blue Ridge Mountains *(above).*
Early settlers named the mountains for the blue haze formed by natural terpenes from the trees. Now hydrocarbons
from automobiles often form a haze, and pollution from many sources threatens the eastern forests.

Photographer: Galen Rowell

> *"Beauty beyond thought everywhere, beneath, above, made and being made forever."*
>
> —JOHN MUIR

CENTRAL CALIFORNIA, U.S.A.

Global 200 Ecoregion #75. In Yosemite Valley, a peaceful dawn unfolds along the Merced River below El Capitan *(left)*, one
of the largest unbroken granite faces in the world. Draining wetlands and building bridges to accommodate the millions of annual
visitors has increased tree growth and altered river flow. While coyotes still hunt its grasslands *(top)* a federal reorganization plan
will attempt to restore much of the valley to its natural state. Most of the 1,169-square-mile national park has been designated a federal
Wilderness Area. Born in Yosemite's heights, the Tuolumne River *(above)* is a Wild and Scenic River. East of Yosemite, a late
afternoon sun lights California gulls *(following pages)* as they wing over briny Mono Lake. Diversion of streams for municipal use in
distant Los Angeles lowered the lake, allowing predators to invade islands and eat the eggs and chicks of the gulls that nested there.
Court action forced a partial refilling of the lake and a restoration of gull protection.

Photographer: Galen Rowell

115

"Wave motion gave life its original direction. It's built into every one of our cells."

—ED RICKETTS

NORTHERN CALIFORNIA, U.S.A.

Global 200 Ecoregion #227. The juncture of sea and land always spells action.
At Big Sur's wild coast in California (*left*), waves and rocks wage a constant thunderous war, highlighted
by spray and foam. Ruddy turnstones (*top*), named for their habit of flipping small rocks to seek food, crowd
the air over a beach. A dunlin (*above*) looks for invertebrates in shallows at Elkhorn Slough.

Photographer: Frans Lanting

MONTEREY, CALIFORNIA, U.S.A.: *Global 200 Ecoregion #227.* Dropping by for a look at the newcomer, a harbor seal *(above)* eyes the photographer in a kelp forest. Perhaps the friendliest of pinnipeds, harbor seals often cavort around human divers. A Pacific green moray eel *(top, right)* allows rock shrimp to cleanse its lumpy skin of debris that might cause infection in a wound. The upwelling of nutrient-rich waters from deep trenches just offshore feeds an elaborate food chain off the California coast. A diver glides among waving branches of kelp *(right).* These most spectacular of the seaweeds can grow to lengths of 200 feet. *Photographer: David Doubilet*

NORTHERN CALIFORNIA, U.S.A.: *Global 200 Ecoregion #227.* Graceful in flight, ponderous at takeoff, a brown pelican *(following pages)* skims the surface of Berkeley's Aquatic Park beside San Francisco Bay, where shorebirds by the hundreds gather in fall and winter. Brown pelicans of the western U.S. remain on the endangered species list, while those on the Atlantic coast, Florida, and Alabama have been removed. *Photographer: Galen Rowell*

KLAMATH-SISKIYOU, NORTHWESTERN U.S.A.

It takes a lot to hush the average tourists, but I saw it happen one morning in the Klamath-Siskiyou forest that straddles California and Oregon. Like me, they walked in silent awe along a well-used trail through the redwoods. The giant trees towered overhead like the spires of cathedrals, while pink rhododendrons beneath them flared in full bloom as fog from the nearby coast wafted by in ghostly clumps. A magical, primeval feeling pervaded the grove, honored by all.

Later that day, I surveyed trackless heights miles inland from any paved road. There in the rain shadow of the coastal mountains, aridity and altitude gradually thinned out the trees. From a high meadow I viewed wave upon wave of forested mountains and couldn't escape the feeling of an earlier, unspoiled era. Just around the corner, however, were miles of checkerboard clearcuts, open sores on the living face of the landscape. Thus, in one single day, the Klamath-Siskiyou had revealed two quite different habitats that had given me two separate soul-stirring moments, as well as two widely divergent visions of environmental protection.

More surprises awaited. Back in the lowlands on another day, I encountered a swamp in the middle of deep forest, where the air smelled dank, ooze sucked at my boots, and carnivorous cobra lilies were devouring living insects.

NORTHERN CALIFORNIA, U.S.A.: *Global 200 Ecoregion #74*. Rhododendrons thrive (*left*) in frequent fog at the feet of old growth redwoods at Del Norte Redwoods State Park, part of the Klamath-Siskiyou forest system. *Photographer: Galen Rowell*

Variety lies at the very core of the Klamath-Siskiyou, where the flora of the Cascades, the Sierra Nevada, and the Coast Ranges meet. The greatest diversity of conifers of any temperate forests in the world is found here. Seventeen conifer species exist within a square mile. The Brewer spruce and Port Orford cedar, unique to these forests, are both survivors of a Pleistocene climate.

Threatened and endangered creatures include the northern spotted owl and the marbled murrelet of the old growth forests, plus the coho salmon and steelhead found in the nation's largest concentration of Wild and Scenic Rivers. Predators include fishers, martens, black bears, mountain lions, and the occasional wolverine. Diversity itself is now endangered, as just 25 percent of the original forest is intact, with only 10 percent of what remains legally protected.

NORTHERN CALIFORNIA, U.S.A.: *Global 200 Ecoregion #74.* The variety of flora found in the Klamath-Siskiyou forests is unmatched in the American West. A wild native western azalea *(left)* brightens the understory. Douglas firs mingle with other conifers *(below)*, a coniferous mix not found in any other of the world's temperate forests. Deadly to small animal life, the rare cobra lily *(bottom, left)* devours insects in soggy areas. More than 1,800 plant species have been recorded in the Klamath-Siskiyou, including 131 that are found nowhere else on Earth.
Photographer: Galen Rowell.

NORTHERN CALIFORNIA, U.S.A.

Global 200 Ecoregion #74. The northern spotted owl *(above)* has been at the center of fierce controversy over the cutting
of old growth forests. Although the threatened bird has become a symbol of conflict between loggers and environmentalists,
other threatened species such as the great gray owl, pileated woodpeckers, and the fisher also depend on mature trees
in the Klamath-Siskiyou. Not endangered, but at home in the Siskiyou Mountains, a mule deer nurses her twin fawns *(right).*
Photographer: Galen Rowell

SAN JUAN ISLANDS, WASHINGTON, U.S.A.

Global 200 Ecoregions #73, #227. Moving northward the sun dips lower in the sky above cool, damp
forests of the Pacific Northwest and beyond, signaling the transition to more extreme climatic conditions
to which wildlife must adjust. The last moments of the day beyond Vancouver Island *(following pages)*
are captured from Mt. Constitution in the San Juan Islands across the Juan de Fuca Strait.
Photographer: Frans Lanting

WASHINGTON, U.S.A.:

Global 200 Ecoregion #73. In Washington's Olympic National Park, maple leaves *(left)* turn color in
the Hoh, one of the few temperate rain forests in the world. Others are in New Zealand, southern Chile, and Japan.
Graced with some 300 inches of rainfall annually, believed the highest in the continental United States,
mosses and ferns carpet the ground in the Hoh's popular hiking area called the Hall of Mosses *(above)*. Rampant plant
growth in some parts of the forest is said to be the greatest weight of living matter, per acre, in the world.

Photographer: Galen Rowell

ALASKA, U.S.A.

Global 200 Ecoregions #73, #141. Mist shrouds the extensive forests and freshwater lakes
and streams of the Kenai Peninsula *(above)*, a wild lobe of land jutting into the Gulf of Alaska.
Along the Teklanika River, a lynx about to pounce on a snowshoe hare stands tall in alpine flowers *(right).*
Dense winter fur shelters it from extreme cold, but has also made it a target of trappers, greatly
depleting its numbers. An international treaty now excludes it from the fur trade.
Photographer: Galen Rowell

ALASKA, U.S.A.

Global 200 Ecoregion #141. Canny carnivore of North America as well as parts of Europe,
Asia, and Africa, a red fox (*left*) hunts in southeast Alaska. It is often observed following grizzly bears,
feasting on scraps they leave behind. Sea otters (*above*) resting on a rocky islet scrutinize the photographer.
They dine on shellfish and fish and eat sea urchins despite the latter's covering of sharp spines.
Photographer: Frans Lanting

ALASKA, U.S.A.: *Global 200 Ecoregion #141*. Braking with wings and tail, a bald eagle (*above*) makes a landing extending stiletto talons that can snatch a fish from water. Pollutants that weakened the shells of their eggs once endangered this avian symbol of the United States, but a ban on DDT has allowed a strong comeback. An Alaskan brown bear (*following pages*) forages in shallows with its cub. The largest carnivores in North America, the big browns can reach ten feet in length and weigh 1,700 pounds. *Photographer: Frans Lanting*

NORTHWEST TERRITORIES, CANADA

Global 200 Ecoregions #85, #116. September twilight accents the full range of changing colors
in dwarf birch beside an Arctic pond *(left)*, hundreds of miles from human settlement along the Thelon River.
The bow-shaped horns of the musk ox *(above)* mark the only survivor of many species of Ice Age oxen
that became extinct in Alaska by 1865, due to human predation. Reintroduced in Alaska, the species
now inhabits the high Arctic across the top of North America and Greenland.
Photographer: Galen Rowell

"Our village life would stagnate if it were not for the forests and meadows that surround it. We need the tonic of wildness."

—HENRY DAVID THOREAU

NORTHWEST TERRITORIES, CANADA

Global 200 Ecoregions #85, #116. Seldom seen and legendarily fierce, a wolverine *(top)* bounds over open tundra. Weighing less than 40 pounds, wolverines will attack full-grown caribou or moose weakened by winter. Although the vast wild spaces in northern Canada gave them some protection, they nearly disappeared in the United States in the early 1900s when trappers sought them for their fur, used in parkas. They are now protected by law in several states. The antlers of a bull caribou of the 480,000-strong Porcupine Herd show red as the animal sheds its velvet *(above)*, a process hastened by rubbing them on bushes. Despite the bloody appearance, shedding causes no pain. Autumn mist fills a low Arctic valley near the Thelon River in The Barrens *(right)*, 250 miles from the nearest road.

Photographer: Galen Rowell

CHURCHILL, MANITOBA, CANADA

Global 200 Ecoregion #116. A polar bear and cubs *(left)* hunker down in a blizzard beside Hudson Bay. Some 300 bears congregate on Cape Churchill each fall to wait for the ice to freeze so they can venture out to hunt seals. Contrary to bears that sleep through the winter, the metabolism of polar bears that live south of the permanent ice pack slows in summer to a state of walking hibernation. Scientists warn that global warming may so extend the ice-free season around Hudson Bay that polar bears won't be able to survive until winter. The arctic fox *(above)* often follows the bears onto pack ice to pick up their leavings.

Photographer: Galen Rowell

"Every organism has reached this moment by threading one needle after another, to survive…against nearly impossible odds."

—EDWARD O. WILSON

PRIBILOF ISLANDS, ALASKA, U.S.A.

Global 200 Ecoregion #235. Dawn silhouettes the craggy roosts of seabirds (*left*) that flock to
the food-rich Bering Sea. Millions of birds, more than 210 species, visit the once-uninhabited volcanic
islands each year. A horned puffin (*top*) rows the air past teeming cliffs, where an enterprising
arctic fox (*above*) stalks a thick-billed murre on a narrow ledge high over the sea.

Photographer: Galen Rowell

PRIBILOF ISLANDS, ALASKA, U.S.A.

Global 200 Ecoregion #235. A young northern fur seal *(right)* practices a dominance display. Some 800,000,
the world's highest concentration of mammals and more than three-quarters of the northern fur seal population, swarm
to the Pribilofs in spring *(above)* to breed and bear young. After early discovery of the Pribilofs' bounty, Russians
relocated Aleut slaves here in the eighteenth century to slaughter millions of the seals for their valuable fur. The commercial
harvest ended in 1984. Today, in a carefully regulated subsistence harvest, the descendants of those Aleut slaves take
only a few young nonbreeding bachelor male seals, which does not endanger the population as a whole.

Photographer: Galen Rowell

BERING STRAIT, SIBERIA: *Global 200 Ecoregion #235.* Both plant and animal life endure in the extreme climate of the subarctic, where the margins of survival are narrow. Storm clouds gather over Arakamchechen Island *(above)* where pristine tundra slopes toward the edge of the sea. Despite the creation of a nature preserve, poaching of Pacific walrus *(top, left)* since the breakup of the Soviet Union cut the population from 15,000 to 3,000 within two years. *Photographer: Galen Rowell*

POINT BARROW, ALASKA, U.S.A.: *Global 200 Ecoregion #235.* A bowhead whale breaches *(left)* in an open lead of the frozen ocean where the Bering Strait meets the Beaufort Sea. Named for their bow-shaped jaws, bowheads feed in the frigid seas in autumn on small crustaceans called copepods. *Photographer: Galen Rowell*

OUTER HEBRIDES, SCOTLAND: *Global 200 Ecoregion #217.* Across the northern subarctic oceans, clown-faced Atlantic puffins *(following pages)* settle on cliffs to nest in spring, chasing small fish underwater to feed their young. They spend entire winters at sea. *Photographer: Frans Lanting*

RED SEA

I once sat underwater with my legs dangling over the edge of the continental shelf as the sea floor dropped away 2,000 feet at the end of the Sinai Peninsula in the Red Sea. Facing south, I turned my head left toward Asia and right toward Africa. This is part of the Great Rift Valley where two huge pieces of the Earth's crust parted company.

Virtually no rain falls on the Red Sea, and no rivers run into it, which accounts for the astonishingly clear water, a diver's delight. Water lost to evaporation is replaced from the Indian Ocean, through the single opening at the Red Sea's southern end. Winds passing over the water cause an upwelling of deep nutrients that feed an impressive marine population. This, the longest, thinnest sea, is the northernmost arm of the Indo-Pacific Ocean that covers most of the Earth.

And what an arm, muscled with some of the most unique creatures anywhere! Here are eels that anchor themselves in the sea floor, anglerfish that lure in prey with a tempting appendage, a goby that acts as eyes for a half-blind shrimp.

Two-inch-long, plankton-eating anthias hang in front of the reefs like veils, and when jacks approach, the whole reef

RED SEA: *Global 200 Ecoregion #201.* In warmer waters of the Middle East a diver floats suspended over beds of soft coral and swarms of anthias along the Ras Mohammed reef off the Sinai Peninsula of Israel (*left*). Clouds of the two-inch anthias and an abundance of other rich reef life feed off plankton elevated from deep canyons by strong surface winds. *Photographer: David Doubilet*

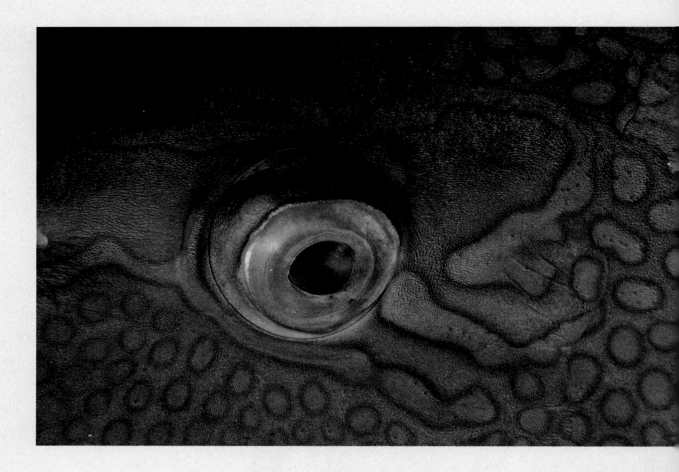

flinches. Big schools of transparent glass fish reflect the sunlight like enormous chandeliers, and they change locations like mercury being poured from one container to another. The steep reef walls themselves resemble a tapestry of different coral species.

Those steep walls also create shadows that extend the twilight, and since many fish become more active at that time of day, it gives me more time to observe them. I've seen sharks mating, fish eating fish, corals wildly feeding. The Red Sea, for me, is a laboratory, a studio, a gallery, a place of real dreams.

RED SEA: *Global 200 Ecoregion #201*. The jeweled eye of the parrot fish *(left)* guides it to dead clumps of stony coral on which it gnaws to consume the worms and small crustaceans living within. Schools of glassy sweepers *(below)* huddle for protection in shaded areas and separate to feed at night. "They move as one," observed the photographer, "and passing through them is like swimming through a waterfall of fish." *Photographer: David Doubilet*

RED SEA: *Global 200 Ecoregion #201*. The homely but huge humphead wrasse *(above)* can grow to 500 pounds, a delicacy so treasured that a meal of it can cost $1,000 in the Far East, endangering its existence. With a mouth as big as a 20-gallon can, it grazes on the reef. Clown fish play among throngs of waving venomous tentacles and the inside-out red skin of the anemone *(above, right)*. As a defense, the clown fish coats itself with the mucus that the anemone secretes to protect itself against its own poison. *Photographer: David Doubilet*

RED SEA: *Global 200 Ecoregion #201*. In branches of black coral the hawkfish *(above)* hovers in ambush, waiting to snatch up juvenile fish with a snap of its forcepslike jaws. In the eyes of other fish the hawkfish's lines break up in camouflage against a linear background. The two-inch lemon goby *(above, right)* prefers stony coral, where it darts in and out of the parapets. Heedless of the reef's clean-up creature, an emperor shrimp *(right)* clambers over a sea cucumber scavenging biological scraps. *Photographer: David Doubilet*

ZAMBEZI RIVER, ZIMBABWE

Global 200 Ecoregion #96. The sun rises behind legendary Victoria Falls *(left)*, first seen by a westerner
in 1855 and named after his queen. The river supports thousands of hippos and crocodiles as it wends between
Zambia and Namibia, touching Botswana on its way to the big Zimbabwean drop.
Photographer: Galen Rowell

SERENGETI, TANZANIA

Global 200 Ecoregion #95. Dawn begins a slow explosion behind an acacia tree *(above)* on this vast plain that is
home to nearly all of Africa's best-known species of large animals, as well as an equal diversity of smaller life forms.
Photographer: Galen Rowell

TANZANIA

Global 200 Ecoregion #95. A mixed herd of zebra and wildebeest *(preceding pages)* grazes in Ngorongoro Crater,
the world's largest volcanic caldera. The 100-square-mile bowl cups within its 2,000-foot wall grasslands and freshwater
pools that feed herds of elephants, hippos, zebras, wildebeests, gazelles, buffalos, ostriches, and some of
the last wild black rhinos in East Africa. The array of herbivores attracts predators such as lions and hyenas.
Photographer: Frans Lanting

Global 200 Ecoregion #95. A hyena feigns disinterest *(above)* to approach a flock of pink flamingos in Ngorongoro Crater.
Perhaps aware of the powerful canine's sudden dashes of the past, the long-legged birds successfully edge away.
Photographer: Galen Rowell

MASAI MARA, KENYA

Global 200 Ecoregion #95. Three lions burst into a mock skirmish *(right)* that lasts
only a few seconds as their pride patrols before dawn.
Photographer: Galen Rowell

CONGO BASIN, DEMOCRATIC REPUBLIC OF CONGO

Global 200 Ecoregion #18. The dense canopy of the central African rain forest *(above)* shelters unique fauna ranging
from okapis to Congo peacocks. Political instability has kept commercial logging to a minimum in the second largest rain forest
in the world after the Amazon. But poachers and farmers threaten the endangered bonobos, or pygmy chimpanzees *(right),* of
the Wamba forest. Our closest primate relatives, they live more peacefully together than common chimpanzees.

Photographer: Frans Lanting

OKAVANGO, BOTSWANA

Astronauts looking down from space say they have seen
Botswana's Okavango Delta as an outstretched green hand
spread over the center of arid southern Africa, highlighted
by fingers of blue. That hand reaching into the vast Kalahari
Desert cups a wild vitality so rich that many have referred
to it as "the last of old Africa," an Eden playing out rhythms
dating back to the Pleistocene.

My view of the world's largest inland delta has been more
intimate, seen while belly down in its warm mud or submerged
in its cool waters to photograph a great menagerie. Elephants
towered over me with rumbling majesty and impalas danced
by nervously, torn between uncertainty and thirst. As I cruised
the labyrinth of channels past walls of tall papyrus, wild-eyed
hippos reared in frightening challenge and Nile crocodiles
glided by like submarines.

Feeding the moist hand that holds back drought are not
one, but two annual gifts of water. One comes from the area's
own wet season, when rains green the Kalahari and allow

OKAVANGO DELTA, BOTSWANA: *Global 200 Ecoregion #105.* Desert grasses
bloom twice annually when rains spread a sheet of water over this flat
land, pumping in new life *(left)*. The delta's own rainy season from
October to March provides a flush of irrigation for vegetation parched
by a long dry season. When that dries months later, a new flood
arrives from rainfall in distant Angolan highlands, transforming grasslands into marshes once again and creating a green haven for large
numbers of African animals. *Photographer: Frans Lanting*

grazers and predators alike to wander far into the surrounding desert. As that bounty grows brittle in the dry months and parched animals cluster around shrinking channels, a second flush of water arrives after a journey of a thousand miles. Rains from the highlands of distant Angola arrive by river and fan out over the delta and into the desert, stimulating new life where existence has become marginal.

Witnessing this drama of individual struggles for survival set against the larger backdrop of landscape and seasonality was the fulfillment of a personal dream. Left to themselves, the animals would play their parts to infinity, but it is the increasing human presence that will determine the fate of the Okavango. However, if the needs of local people and the economic hopes of a developing country can somehow be balanced with respect for wildlife, this jewel in the desert can be a beacon for a New Africa.

OKAVANGO DELTA, BOTSWANA: *Global 200 Ecoregion #105.* Reaching top speeds of 70 miles per hour does not guarantee that a cheetah, resting with its cubs *(left),* can outrun civilization. Extinct in India where they once roamed, endangered in Africa by farmlands that encroach on the open spaces they require, and poached for their spotted fur, the sleek cats border on extinction. Ample rains return lush vegetation to cheetah habitat in the Makgadikgadi grasslands *(below). Photographer: Frans Lanting*

OKAVANGO DELTA, BOTSWANA

Global 200 Ecoregion #105. Dry season in the delta region drives elephants north to flood plains
of the Chobe River *(left)*, where they find water in streams and small swamps. Loss of habitat presents
the greatest threat to adults, each of whom require up to 300 pounds of forage a day. In search of
greener pastures, a herd moves through the Mopane woodlands *(above)*.

Photographer: Frans Lanting

OKAVANGO DELTA, BOTSWANA

Global 200 Ecoregion #105. Saline fingers reach across the Makgadikgadi salt flats *(right)*.
Once a large lake, the area dried up when subterranean shifts altered the course of the rivers that fed it. Now irregular
rains occasionally bring hordes of flamingoes that feed here while the water lasts. Dealing with drought in their
own immobile way, baobab trees *(above)* store water in swollen trunks or fleshy leaves. Elephants forage on the fibrous
bark in hard times, and the trees provide homes to many species. Baobab trunks can grow thirty feet thick.
Photographer: Frans Lanting

ALDABRA ATOLL: *Global 200 Ecoregion #200.* East of Tanzania rises a platform in the sea,
Cosmoledo Island *(above)*, barely breaking the surface of the Indian Ocean. Too small for development,
the Aldabra Islands have remained an unspoiled laboratory of reef life. Beyond a lone shrub left on
a hillock at low tide *(top, right)* appears a fringe of mangrove, breeding ground for the entire population
of Indian Ocean frigate birds. Green waters of the lagoon reflect in the undersides of the clouds.
The isolated islands have also provided a haven for giant tortoises. With a mating ritual almost like
a kiss *(right)*, a male and female affirm each other's identities. *Photographer: David Doubilet*

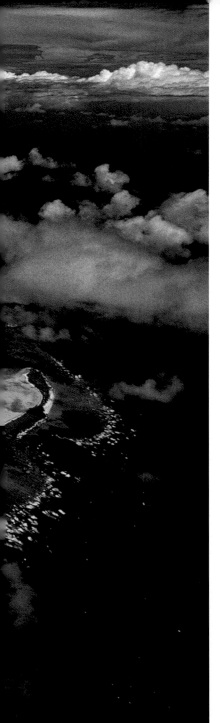

ALDABRA ATOLL

Global 200 Ecoregion #200. A batfish the size of a dinner plate *(left)* plays around
the anchor line of a dive boat. A school of one-spots *(above)*, each five inches long,
presents an underwater lottery for predators. The only defense: safety in numbers.
Photographer: David Doubilet

MADAGASCAR

Global 200 Ecoregion #131. South of Aldabra on the 1,000-mile-long island of Madagascar a ring-tailed
lemur stands tall *(left)* to reach a meal of berries. Primates like humans, lemurs evolved into at least thirty-two species
and fifty subspecies when the island drifted away from Africa millions of years ago. Additional species continue
to be found. Although the moist forests preferred by most lemurs line Madagascar's east coast, savanna and scrub prevail
over the island and the southern tip is ringed by spiny desert *(above)*. Lemur habitat is shrinking as an exploding
human population burns forests to create croplands. Four-fifths of Madagascar now lies barren.
Photographer: Frans Lanting

MADAGASCAR: *Global 200 Ecoregion #58.* Voyageurs on the evolutionary raft that was Madagascar benefited as it separated from the African mainland 165 million years ago. Castaways include a chameleon *(above)*, whose pigment changes colors with its moods. Half the world's chameleon species live on the island. Isolation meant safety for lemurs such as these sifakas *(right)*, huddling in a tamarind tree. Few predators, and no other primates, managed to float on vegetation across the widening gulf between Madagascar and the rest of the African continent. Humans arrived around A.D. 500, and within the next thousand years, fourteen species of lemurs became extinct, including some the size of great apes. Preservation efforts and the creation of national parks have slightly improved the fortunes of wildlife. Human economies might be improved as well by tourists coming to see biological oddities that include the octopus tree *(following pages)*, bristling with thorns but unrelated to any cactus. *Photographer: Frans Lanting*

NEPAL: *Global 200 Ecoregion #68.* Far north of Madagascar and far higher in elevation, the bright shoulders of 22,943-foot Machapuchare, "the fish's tail" *(above)*, loom above dark cloud forest in the Himalayas. Sacred to locals, the mountain lies within the 1,000-square-mile Annapurna Conservation Area, created in 1987 by WWF and the government of Nepal to empower the local people to protect habitat while living off the land. The amazing diversity of terrain ranges from 26,000-foot summits to the world's deepest canyon, the Kali Gandaki, and from rain forests in the south to treeless steppes in the north. The innovative conservation project has become a global model for Third World preservation of natural environment. *Photographer: Galen Rowell*

NEPAL

Global 200 Ecoregions #67, #97. Rhododendrons bloom at 10,000 feet *(left)* in the Kanchenjunga Conservation Area, patterned by WWF after the Annapurna Conservation Area, which was created a decade earlier. Kanchenjunga, the world's third highest mountain, straddles the borders of Nepal, India, and China. The three governments are working to create trinational reserves on all sides. In the Royal Chitwan National Park southwest of Kathmandu, where all rivers feed into the Ganges and wildlife thrives in protected habitat, ecotourists on Asian elephants *(above)* from Tiger Tops Lodge view a one-horned Indian rhinoceros and its calf.

Photographer: Galen Rowell

"*Every country needs wilderness where people can go—young and old—to have a renewal of spirit.*"
—SIR EDMUND HILLARY

NEPAL

Global 200 Ecoregion #67. Ama Dablam *(right)*, seen from 13,000 feet above Khumjung, is generally considered far more beautiful than neighboring Mt. Everest. Sunset on the 22,493-foot peak silhouettes a Himalayan blue pine, a common tree of these middle-level forests. Collision between the Indian subcontinent and Eurasia pushed up the spectacular Himalayan range. Among the wild residents of the range's upper-level forests, the highly endangered musk deer *(top)* gets its name from a musk gland that sells as an aphrodisiac for up to three times its weight in gold. With protection in Sagarmatha National Park, the population of Himalayan tahr *(above)* is now rapidly expanding. These wild goats are easy prey for the now-rare snow leopard, Himalayan wolf, and Asiatic brown bear.

Photographer: Galen Rowell

TIBET

You cannot thirst for adventures in high places, as I have for most of my life, without dreaming of going to Tibet. Rightfully called the "roof of the world," the Tibetan Plateau is laced by great mountains that give birth to many of the great rivers of Asia. Its valleys range from 12,000 to 16,000 feet.

Until recently, such loftiness kept Tibet in isolation. It was a rugged, forbidding place, where time stood still and Buddhist people developed a deep spiritual regard for all land and beings. Nearly every explorer who had ventured to Tibet reported trekking amid herds of gazelle and wild ass that mingled with their caravans.

In 1981, my first of six trips to Tibet was a great adventure but a major wildlife disappointment. In the thirty years since the Tibetans had lost control of their homeland, the forests had been leveled and the wildlife nearly eliminated—hunted for food or illegal trade. Native herbivores had been replaced with domestic livestock. For two months I hiked and climbed in spectacular mountains where wildlife was absent. I also drove

---

TIBETAN PLATEAU: *Global 200 Ecoregion #114.* Thin air does not slow Tibetan wild ass (*left*) as they gallop across a plain near the border between Tibet Autonomous Region and Nepal. At 15,000 feet, the kiang, as they are called in Tibetan, can run at 35 miles per hour for more than half an hour. Once common all across the Tibetan Plateau, their numbers have been greatly reduced by hunting and displaced by domestic livestock. This herd lives in an extremely rugged and remote part of western Tibet. *Photographer: Galen Rowell*

over a thousand miles of dirt roads on the Tibetan side of Mount Everest without seeing a single large wild mammal.

Subsequent travels led me into the remote high steppes of western Tibet, where I found hidden valleys with herds of wild ass, gazelle, and antelope. I also discovered subsistence nomads living in remote regions. My photographs so excited the Dalai Lama that he agreed to write a book using my images to focus on his homeland's enduring cultural and natural heritage. In *My Tibet* His Holiness states his dream that "the entire Tibetan Plateau will someday be transformed into a true peace sanctuary . . . the world's largest national park or biosphere."

While some animals—such as the wild yak, giant panda, and argali sheep—are uniquely Tibetan, others are more familiar, with good reason. The plateau is a remnant of the Palearctic life zone that circled the upper latitudes during the ice ages. Tibetan wolves, foxes, and bears are thus closely related to their kin across America and Europe—solid links in the fragile chain of global biodiversity.

TIBET: *Global 200 Ecoregion #114.* The endangered black-necked crane *(left)* shows its colors against a spur of Shishapangma, the only one of the world's fourteen 26,000-foot peaks wholly in Tibet. Loss of habitat and poaching have reduced the population of this high marsh dweller. A ghostly cat rapidly fading from the roof of the world, the snow leopard *(below)* has been a victim of the quest for its beautiful fur, and the loss of its prey species to hunting and competition for grazing. *Photographer: Galen Rowell*

"Our wild animals are a symbol of freedom. Without them something is missing from even the most beautiful landscape."

—DALAI LAMA

TIBET

Global 200 Ecoregion #114. Like a cloud-wreathed fantasy, the 24,000-foot Kangbochen (*left*) looms over a quiet
stream meandering through a valley. Dwellers of the heights, blue sheep (*top*) traverse a cliff below holy Mount Kailas,
Earthly representation of the center of the universe for Buddhists, Hindus, Jains, and Bonpos—followers
of the original Tibetan religion before the arrival of Buddhism. The Tibetan argali (*above*) has the heaviest horns of
mountain sheep found anywhere—up to 65 pounds. Seldom seen anymore, it lives at altitudes up to 18,000 feet.
Photographer: Galen Rowell

BORNEO

To walk through a forest in Borneo is like being in a laboratory of life itself. Straddling the tropics in the Malay Archipelago, it is drenched by as much as 200 inches of rain a year. When the rain stops, the sunlight pours in, creating the steamy conditions that nurture an extravagance of life-forms.

More tree species can be found in twenty-five acres of Borneo rain forest than in all of North America. More bird species live in Borneo than in all of Europe, and as many mammals as in all of Australia. Reptiles and amphibians abound, and only a fraction of the millions of insect species have even been identified.

Although I have visited many strongholds of nature around the world, I was astonished at the ingenuity of life that manifests itself in Borneo. A lizard with a striped tail and a delicate fringe lining its back rears like a miniature dinosaur. Some 1,200 different species of orchids ornament Borneo's montane forests. Big-eyed tarsiers cling to tree branches like knobby-fingered goblins. Broadbills flit through the air like

SABAH, BORNEO: *Global 200 Ecoregions #40, #41*. South nearly to the equator, a rain forest shrouded in mist shows gaps from logging activity *(left)*. Although part of the Sabah rain forest remains intact, most of the rain forest in Borneo has been shredded into small remnants. Two recent El Niños have added to the destruction of species-rich habitat by drying the jungle into fuel for forest fires. Peat beneath the forest floor makes them difficult to extinguish as burns smolder undetected for days before blazing forth again. *Photographer: Frans Lanting*

emeralds on wings. Orangutans swing placidly through the trees as if offering themselves as a new and mellower hominid. The night air vibrates with a constant hum as if the very darkness breathes on its own.

Much of this rain forest world is changing fast. It holds valuable trees that fuel the economies of Malaysia and Indonesia, which share the tear-shaped island along with tiny Brunei. Whether a new awareness of the larger treasures the forests hold can balance out the threats is uncertain. But I do believe we need this tropical laboratory of life as a storehouse for our future.

SABAH, BORNEO: *Global 200 Ecoregions #40, #41*. A deeply cut gorge and tall straight trees *(below)* in the Danum Valley Conservation Area reveal a slice of the wild Borneo that once prevailed. Rainfall up to 200 inches a year and constant warmth feed luxuriant growth and unusual life-forms. In this hotbed of biodiversity twenty-five acres of rain forest may hold more tree species than all of North America. More varieties of birds live here than in all Europe, and more mammals than in Australia. Butterflies renowned for both their size and beauty feast on blossoms, including the gemlike Rajah Brooke's bird wing *(left)*. *Photographer: Frans Lanting*

SABAH, BORNEO

Global 200 Ecoregions #40, #41. With motherly patience, an orangutan watches over the tree limb antics of
an infant *(left)*. Highly dependent on their mothers, young orangutans do not forage on their own for six or seven years.
The name *orangutan*, in Malay, means "man of the forest." Using long arms that droop nearly to the ground when
they stand upright, orangutans spend more time in the trees than do their African relatives, chimpanzees and gorillas.
Among the reptiles and amphibians adapted to varying heights of the rain forest canopy, the flying frog *(above)*
can glide on widely webbed feet from one level to another.
Photographer: Frans Lanting

SABAH, BORNEO: *Global 200 Ecoregions #40, #41.* Munching its way through dense forest, a Sumatran rhinoceros wears caked red mud from its last wallow *(left)*. Smallest of the five species of rhino, it stands barely four feet tall at the shoulder, compared to six and a half feet for the African white rhino. Few Sumatran rhinos remain in Borneo's shrinking forests. Among the smallest primates is the tarsier *(above)*, a chipmunk-sized tree dweller with enormous eyes that help it see in the dark to catch insects and small lizards. To jump to another branch, the tarsier uncoils its long, powerful legs, springs off backward, and turns its body around for a landing elsewhere. *Photographer: Frans Lanting*

209

SULU/SULAWESI SEAS, INDONESIA, MALAYSIA AND PHILIPPINES: *Global 200 Ecoregions #207, #208*. Meadows of coral line the shallow sea floor *(preceding pages)* near the island of Alor off southeastern Indonesia. Coral reefs abounding in the warm waters contain an astounding diversity of jewelled species, at risk as the fifth most populous nation on Earth continues to gain more people. The volcanic island of Manado Tua rises like a slouch hat above the sea *(above)* as fishermen venture forth in canoes. The rising population overfishes the reefs, which, despite their rich and colorful coral life, do not offer a vast source of human food. The deadly harvest includes poisoning the water with cyanide and blasting with explosives, destructive to all underwater life. Still unaffected, a yellow-masked angelfish *(top, right)* grazes on the reefs as a small valet, an inch-long shrimp, rides along on the arm of a starfish *(right)*, vacuuming detritus off its host. *Photographer: David Doubilet*

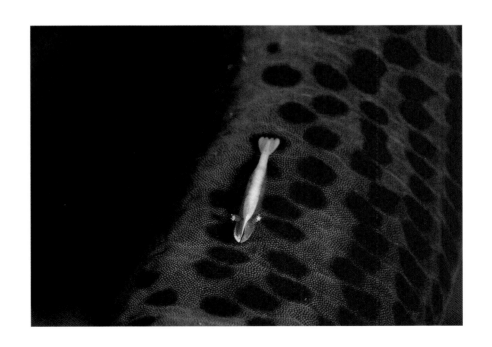

PALAU: *Global 200 Ecoregion #211.* Northeast of Indonesia biology begets geology where sponges bore into coral-based islands, allowing them to be undercut by wave erosion. Diver Kelly Ward swims near one *(right)* that appears ready to fly into space. At least 300 species of coral flourish in the 93-mile-long string of Palau Islands, creating stony communities alive with fish, crustaceans, and mollusks. In death, the corals leave their limestone exoskeletons that eventually bloom with plant life when they extend above the water. At Seventy Islands National Park *(above)*, the tips of ancient reefs reach above the surface in random polygons, furred by vegetation. *Photographer: David Doubilet*

PALAU

Global 200 Ecoregion #211. Haunting a landlocked lagoon, a wraithlike jellyfish *(left)* three feet long
drifts beneath a bright sun. Rims of reefs that thrust above the sea at the edges of islands form lakes of salt water,
unconnected by open channels to the ocean but recharged by seawater surging through the porous limestone
and through tunnels connected to lagoons. Developed in isolation, these jellyfish are found nowhere else. Free of
predators, they have lost their sting, allowing marine biologist Dr. William Hamner to swim through a swarm *(above)*
without pain in a lagoon called Jellyfish Lake. At night they descend to feed on bottom-dwelling bacteria; by day they rise
near the surface where the sun converts the ingested bacteria into energy. The unique lakes have developed their
own individual communities, sometimes with only two species, sometimes with the full range of reef life. In the darkness
of the tunnels grow colorful corals that receive no sunlight, but thrive on nutrients that surge in with the tides.
Photographer: David Doubilet

PAPUA NEW GUINEA

All coral reefs are magical, and different in their own way. I would never prefer one over the other, but if I were asked to choose one place where I would like to explore more, it would be Papua New Guinea. This island, part of the western tropical Pacific, has the most complex island geography in the world. There are deep lagoons, steep reefs, and volcanoes.

Imagine the richest of seas touching the edge of one of the largest islands covered with dense rain forest. The result is the coral reefs off Papua New Guinea, where nutrients drain from the land into the water and feed a rainbow of marine species.

The waters are Eden-like, the variety astounding. Seventeen species of clownfish nestle among stinging anemones for safety from predators. There are twenty types of butterfly fish, and fifteen groupers instead of the six found in other warm seas—fish that live on hundreds of species of corals. This is not a mere tapestry of life; it is an extremely complex and overdecorated apartment.

PAPUA NEW GUINEA: *Global 200 Ecoregion #210.* The richest of all coral reefs are found south of Palau along the coast of Papua New Guinea. Dawn silhouettes a green tree coral near the island of New Ireland, as two surgeon fish fly past *(left).* A swift current flowing through the Planet Channel leaves the water surface glassy smooth, giving the corals and fish the look of a surface scene against a cloudy sky. Unparalleled diversity in these waters stems from a lowering of the oceans during the ice age. Species evolved in basins elsewhere then converged here when the water levels rose again. *Photographer: David Doubilet*

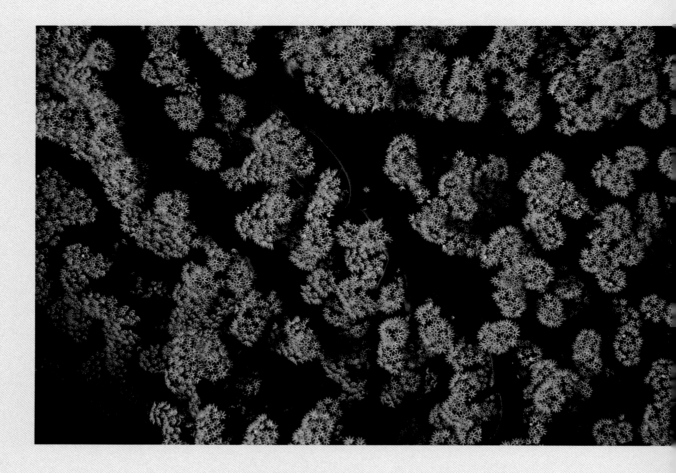

The huge variety of species can be traced to the region's geology. Here at the western edge of the Ring of Fire, volcanism created a number of huge basins on the sea floor. When the ice age locked up much of the planet's water and lowered the sea level, the basins became miniature oceans. Many separate species evolved in them. When the ocean levels rose again, those species spread out and mingled at Papua New Guinea, the gathering place of the world's great oceans and a cornucopia of nutrients.

There are creatures of intense design—fish with checkerboard patterns and fish that look like football jerseys. Coral reefs are the jewels of our oceans, and the untouched waters of Papua New Guinea are the richest of them all.

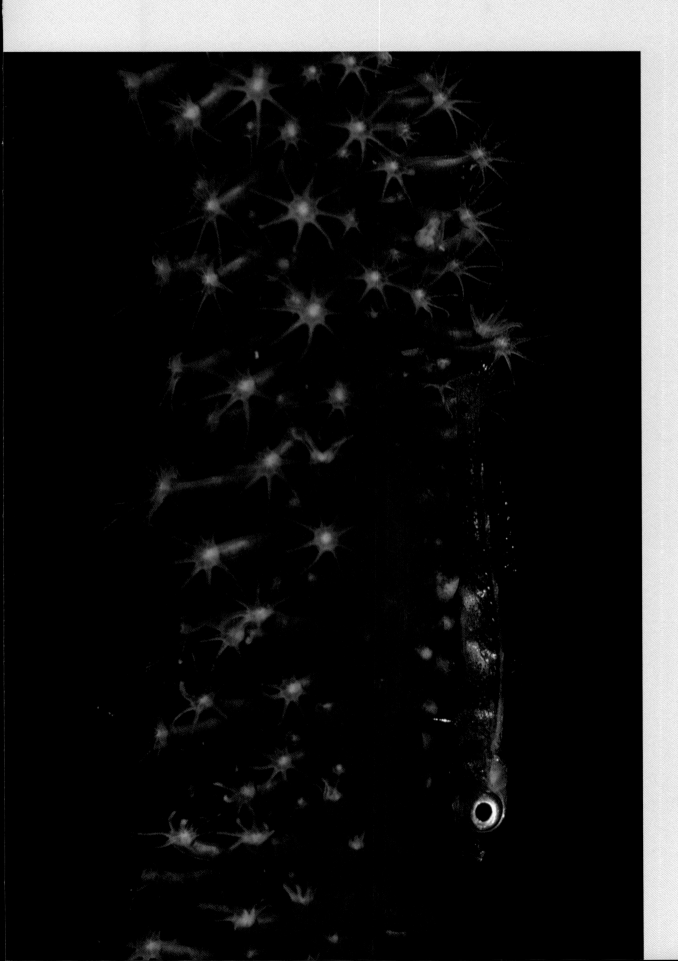

PAPUA NEW GUINEA: *Global 200 Ecoregion #210.* Fish or coral? Small victims find out when the completely camouflaged scorpionfish *(above)* snatches them for a meal. Woe as well to the diver who comes in painful contact with the venomous dorsal and anal spines giving the fish its name. Also hard to detect, a small goby *(right)* blends perfectly into the patterns of a sponge, which it serves by cleaning the larger animal's outer surface. Elaborate nostrils on the thumb-size head of a blue ribbon eel *(top, right)* signal the slightest movement of approaching predator or prey. *Photographer: David Doubilet*

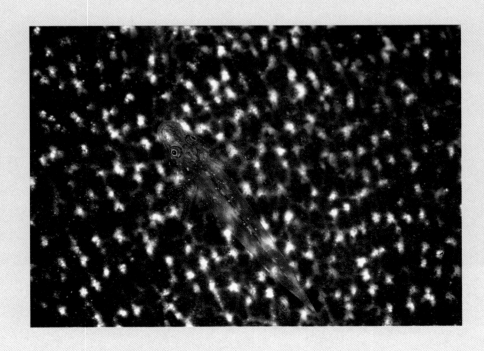

COASTAL AUSTRALIA

Global 200 Ecoregion #214. Farther south along the eastern coast of Australia lies the longest coral system in
the world, the Great Barrier Reef. Not a single, solid reef, it is interlaced with passages along its 1,250-mile length from
the tip of Cape York to two-thirds the way down the state of Queensland. River within the sea, a long, deep channel
just off Hamilton Island splits the Hook and Hardy Reefs (*left*), most spectacular of the reef system. Through branches of
gorgonian coral (*above*) swims a small school of anthias. In the cooler waters of South Australia, a sixteen-foot
great white shark (*following pages*) cruises near the appropriately named Dangerous Reef, where it feeds mostly on sea lions.
Hooked by sports fishermen, shot by lobstermen and tuna farmers, the great whites have few friends except those
who worry about its continued existence as the most spectacular of sharks.

Photographer: David Doubilet

SOUTHERN AUSTRALIA: *Global 200 Ecoregion #232.* Limestone rocks shaped by breakers and known as the Twelve Apostles *(above)* receive a benediction from the setting sun near the border with Victoria State. Here, cold waters from the deep meet with warm waters from the mainland on a broad continental shelf, home to a galaxy of sea creatures normally found at much lower depths. Among them, the foot-long leafy sea dragon *(top, right)* with its trailing appendages seems to be wearing camouflage. Of similar size but seeming like a fanciful beast from a children's fable, the weedy sea dragon *(right)* appears ready to snort fire. Both are distant cousins of the sea horse. *Photographer: David Doubilet*

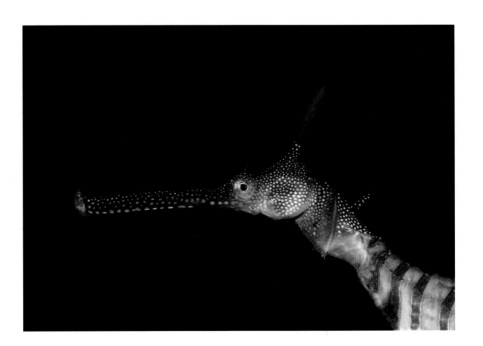

CENTRAL AUSTRALIA

Global 200 Ecoregion #137. Red sand and rocks mark the rugged interior of Australia *(left)*, where but few of
the hardiest of humans and wildlife can survive. Native animal species that survive with little impact on the land
include the red kangaroo *(above)*, one of Australia's many marsupials. The continent holds by far the greatest number
of these mammals that deliver their young prematurely and nurture them inside a pouch instead of inside the womb.
Photographer: Frans Lanting

TASMANIA, AUSTRALIA: *Global 200 Ecoregion #71.* Once part of a supercontinent called Gondwana that broke up 130 million years ago, Australia wandered alone for 65 million years, developing its own menagerie of marsupials. Its southernmost state of Tasmania became an ark for a few species not found elsewhere after rising seas separated it from the mainland. Among the survivors in Tasmania's isolation, the roly-poly wombat *(top, right)* lives in burrows and emerges only at night. Then it becomes prey for the Tasmanian devil *(right)*, a pouched predator with a hauntingly canine appearance. Long, tapered leaves of pandani plants *(above)* offer evidence of the long-ago breakup of Gondwana. Close relatives of the saggy-leafed pandani "screw pines" as well as primitive King Billy pines and nothofagus beech have been found in the flora or fossils of Australia, New Zealand, Africa, Antarctica, and India, indicating all were once part of a single huge land mass. *Photographer: Galen Rowell*

LORD HOWE ISLAND: *Global 200 Ecoregion #216*. East of Australia, damselfish, wrasse, and sergeant-majors swirl just below the surface (*top, left*), within sight of a volcanic dot of land in the southern Pacific. Here warm currents from the equator bathe Earth's southernmost coral reef at the edge of the chilly Tasman Sea. Blue-tinged in a blue world, a wrasse speeds past (*left*). *Photographer: David Doubilet*

FRENCH POLYNESIA: *Global 200 Ecoregion #215*. In a sprinkling of small islands scattered across the South Pacific, a black-tipped shark (*above*), near the limits of its domain, cruises a shallow lagoon at Rangiroa, largest island in the archipelago. Bold in its search for prey, it will swim after smaller fish that seek protection near shore until its back protrudes above water. *Photographer: David Doubilet*

FRENCH POLYNESIA: *Global 200 Ecoregion #215.* Reflected by the water's surface, three-inch-long baby green turtles *(above)* indicate a healthy ocean, as they swim in a clear lagoon at Marutea. Peril in the form of a host of predators awaits them when they cross the coral reef into deep water. Among the survivors, females will return years later to lay eggs in the sand, an instinctive breeding pattern now often complicated by beachfront development. Males never touch land again. *Photographer: David Doubilet*

"...*each created thing is adapted to the place for which it was intended.*"

—CHARLES DARWIN

HAWAIIAN ISLANDS, U.S.A.

Global 200 Ecoregion #53. Thousands of miles north of French Polynesia, the volcanic mountain Waialeale on the island
of Kauai *(left)* wears a cloak of green over erosion deeply cut by heavy rainfall. Spawned in the emptiness of the Pacific 2,500 miles
from the nearest continent, the Hawaiian Islands gained life from any transient bird, seed, or mat of vegetation that flew
or floated their way. Whatever took hold flourished in splendid isolation. Eden ended with the arrival of humans about 1,500 years
ago, with competitive plants and a scourge of new animals. As a result, more specially adapted species have been lost
in Hawaii than in all North America. A native with leaves sometimes three feet wide, the Apé Apé plant *(top)* can serve as
an umbrella in a rainstorm. The taro plant provides a beneficial habitat for a visiting stilt *(above)*.

Photographer: Frans Lanting

HAWAIIAN LEEWARD ISLANDS, U.S.A.: *Global 200 Ecoregion #215.* Flight training for Laysan albatross chicks *(left)* begins with stretching their wings and feeling the wind beneath them. As adults, they will roam the North Pacific only to return eventually to their nesting stronghold, these flat remnants of land created by the same volcanic action that later raised today's main Hawaiian Islands. On one of the older, eroded Leewards, a green sea turtle comes ashore to nest *(above). Photographer: Frans Lanting*

HAWAIIAN ISLANDS, U.S.A.

Global 200 Ecoregion #53. Brilliant specimens in the evolutionary laboratory called Hawaii include the silversword *(right)*,
which manages to survive in barren landscape at 11,000 feet. Descendent of a relative of the American daisy, its seeds probably arrived
in the plumage of a bird. Once nearly wiped out by introduced goats and careless visitors, it now recovers under vigorous protection.
Newcomers wiped out many relatives of the honeycreeper known as the i'iwi *(above)*, whose curved bill adapted to sip nectar
from a lobelia blossom that has the same shape. More than a hundred honeycreepers evolved from a single species that arrived here
by chance. Avian malaria transmitted by introduced mosquitoes has been devastating to much of Hawaii's bird life.
Photographer: Frans Lanting

HAWAIIAN LEEWARD ISLANDS, U.S.A.: *Global 200 Ecoregion #53.* A flat beach in the Hawaiian Leewards is the final sanctuary for a monk seal and its pup (*above*). This species of primitive pinniped, which lacks the large flippers of other seals, is one of the most endangered animals on Earth. There are also some extremely endangered groups of monk seals in the Mediterranean. *Photographer: Frans Lanting*

> "…Here, nature was at her mightiest…wild as any land on our globe, it lies unseen and untrodden."
>
> —ROALD AMUNDSEN

ANTARCTICA

Global 200 Ecoregion # 233. South to the frigid ends of the Earth lies an Eden of creatures adapted to a severe climate.
A pair of emperor penguins (*left*) reassert their bond with a series of bows and flutelike calls. In colonies of thousands, they reunite
after foraging at sea by recognizing voice prints in each other's haunting cries. The only two flowering plants that exist on the
continent are Antarctic pink and a type of bundle grass (*top*), which share the same fertile niche just above tide line. Survival of both
species depends on the right combination of fresh water from glacial melt and a wind-sheltered spot facing the sun. In the more
amenable subantarctic, king penguins (*above*) share arctic tundra of the Salisbury Plain on South Georgia Island.
Photographer: Galen Rowell

ANTARCTICA: *Global 200 Ecoregion #233.* A flock of pintado petrels *(above)* swoops past an iceberg near the tip of the Antarctic Peninsula. Distant relatives of the albatross, they range around the entire Antarctic and venture as far northward as two-thirds of the way to the equator. Banking in a blizzard *(top, right),* a lone petrel displays the remarkable camouflage that matches the color of sea foam on dark water. When seen from below, its pale belly blends with the sky. Sociable to humans but a menace to penguins and seals, extremely intelligent orcas *(right)* cruise the icy waters of Paradise Bay. On South Georgia Island, a river runs through a forest of king penguins *(following pages),* a colony of some 200,000. Their quiet proximity to each other, even more pronounced in the winter huddles of emperor penguins, stands as a model of peaceful coexistence on an increasingly crowded planet. *Photographer: Galen Rowell*

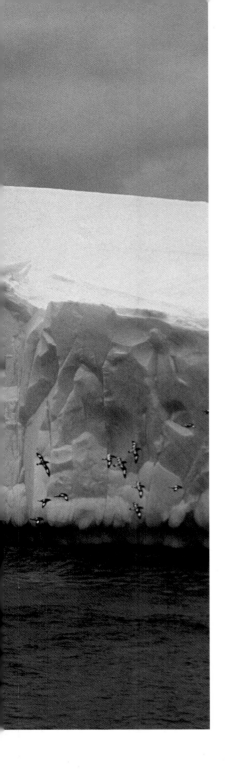

THE GLOBAL 200

PRESERVING A RICH TAPESTRY OF THE EARTH'S MOST OUTSTANDING WILDLIFE HABITATS

The current extinction crisis requires dramatic action to save the tremendous variety of life on Earth. Most conservation biologists recognize that although we cannot save everything, we should at least ensure that the earth's major ecosystem and habitat types be represented in strategies to protect wildlife habitats.

The Global 200 is the first attempt to achieve representation of all major habitat types at a global scale. WWF's primary objective is to promote the conservation of terrestrial, freshwater, and marine ecosystems harboring globally important biological diversity and ecological processes. The Global 200 addresses this goal by identifying the world's most outstanding examples within each major habitat type (e.g., tropical dry forests, large lakes, coral reefs).

The representation approach, accepted by a growing number of conservationists, is soundly based in conservation biology. It integrates the goal of maintaining species diversity (the traditional focus of biodiversity conservation) with another level of conservation action, the preservation of distinct ecosystems and ecological processes. While it is true that more than half of all species are likely to occur in the world's tropical moist forests, the other half of all species are found elsewhere.

Although conservation action typically takes place at the country level, patterns of biodiversity and ecological processes (e.g., migration) often do not conform to political boundaries. Thus, we used ecoregions as the unit of analysis in creating the Global 200. An ecoregion is a relatively large unit of land or water containing a characteristic set of natural communities that shares a large majority of their species, dynamics, and environmental conditions.

To maintain representation of biodiversity at a global scale, we first stratified ecoregions by realm (terrestrial, freshwater, and marine), then further divided realms by major habitat types (MHTs) that describe different areas of the world that share similar environmental conditions, habitat structure, and patterns of biological complexity (e.g., beta diversity), and that contain communities with similar guild structures and species adaptations. We identified twelve terrestrial MHTs, three freshwater ones, and four marine MHTs. Each MHT was further subdivided biogeographically (e.g., Nearctic, Indian Ocean) in order to represent unique faunas and floras of different continents or ocean basins. Finally, we identified ecoregions within each biogeographic realm that represent the most distinctive examples of biodiversity for a given MHT.

We identified 237 ecoregions whose biodiversity and representation values are outstanding at a global scale. They represent the terrestrial, freshwater, and marine realms, and the nineteen MHTs nested within these realms. Among the three realms, 59 percent are terrestrial, 15 percent are freshwater ecoregions, and 26 percent are marine. Terrestrial ecoregions outnumber those of the other realms largely because there is more localized endemism in terrestrial than in marine biotas.

The data used to establish the ecoregions of the Global 200 was taken from intensive regional and global analyses of biodiversity patterns undertaken by WWF's Conservation Science Program and numerous other organizations and individuals. Assessments of the data were conducted in collaboration with hundreds of regional experts and included extensive literature reviews.

The ecoregions of the Global 200 vary greatly not only in their biological distinctiveness, but also in their conservation status. Among terrestrial Global 200 ecoregions, 47 percent are considered critical or endangered, 29 percent vulnerable, and 24 percent relatively stable or intact. In ecoregions that have been dramatically altered, characteristic species and communities survive only in the few remaining small blocks of habitat. Among the terrestrial MHTs, ecoregions falling within the tropical dry forests, temperate grasslands, Mediterranean shrublands, and temperate broadleaf forests are the most threatened. Island ecoregions are projected to experience a wave of extinctions over the next two decades given the fragility of island ecosystems, the sensitivity and endemicity of island species, and the severe threats native island biotas face worldwide from introduced species and habitat loss.

One concern of the Global 200 approach to biodiversity conservation is that it is ambitious, and that by focusing on 237 ecoregions rather than on a handful of "hot spots" or areas of highly concentrated biodiversity, we run the risk of placing less emphasis on the most diverse and distinct ecoregions. In response, we argue that the broad geographic reach of the Global 200 makes almost every nation on Earth a stakeholder in a global conservation strategy. From the global scale to regional- and national-level conservation strategies, the Global 200 lends weight to shared priorities and provides a global perspective for local, regional, and global conservation action.

—Eric Dinerstein and David M. Olson

Note: This is a summary of a more comprehensive document, "The Global 200: A representation approach to conserving the Earth's distinctive ecoregions" by D.M. Olson and E. Dinerstein. This document is available on the Internet at http://www.worldwildlife.org.

Conservation Science Program
World Wildlife Fund–U.S.
1250 24th St. NW
Washington, D.C. 20037, U.S.A.

GLOBAL 200 ECOREGIONS

TERRESTRIAL ECOREGIONS

TROPICAL & SUBTROPICAL MOIST BROADLEAF FORESTS
Neotropical
1. Greater Antillean Moist Forests - Haiti, Cuba, Dominican Republic, Jamaica, Puerto Rico
2. Talamancan & Isthmian Pacific Forests - Costa Rica, Panama
3. Chocó-Darién Moist Forests - Colombia, Panama, Ecuador
4. Northern Andean Montane Forests - Ecuador, Colombia, Venezuela, Peru
5. Coastal Venezuela Montane Forests - Venezuela
6. Guianan Moist Forests - Guyana, Suriname, French Guiana, Brazil, Venezuela
7. Napo Moist Forests - Ecuador, Colombia, Peru
8. Rio Negro-Juruá Moist Forests - Colombia, Brazil, Peru, Venezuela
9. Guyanan Highlands Moist Forests - Guyana, Venezuela, Brazil
10. Varzea Flooded Forests - Peru, Brazil, Venezuela, Ecuador, Colombia
11. Andean Yungas - Ecuador, Colombia, Venezuela, Bolivia, Peru, Argentina
12. Southwestern Amazonian Moist Forests - Peru, Brazil, Bolivia
13. Atlantic Forests - Brazil, Paraguay, Argentina
Afrotropical
14. Guinean Moist Forests - Ghana, Guinea, Ivory Coast, Liberia, Sierra Leone, Togo, Benin
15. Congolian Coastal Forests - Cameroon, Gabon, R. Congo, Nigeria, Benin, D.R. Congo
16. Gulf of Guinea Islands Forests - São Tomé & Príncipe, Equatorial Guinea
17. Western Congo Basin Forests - Central African Republic, Cameroon, R. Congo
18. Northeastern Congo Basin Forests - D.R. Congo, Central African Republic, Sudan
19. Southern Congo Basin Forests - D.R. Congo, R. Congo, Angola
20. East African Montane Forests - Kenya, Tanzania
21. Albertine Rift Highland Forests - D.R. Congo, Rwanda, Uganda, Burundi, Tanzania
22. Angolan Afromontane Forests - Angola
23. East African Coastal Forests - Tanzania, Kenya, Mozambique, Somalia
24. Eastern Arc Montane Forests - Tanzania, Kenya
25. Madagascar Moist Forests - Madagascar
Indo-Malayan
26. Western Ghats Moist Forests - India
27. Sri Lankan Moist Forests - Sri Lanka
28. Northern Indochina Subtropical Moist Forests - Myanmar, Thailand, Laos
29. Southeast China Subtropical Forests - China
30. Taiwan Montane Forests - Taiwan
31. Annamite Range Moist Forests - Laos, Vietnam, Thailand
32. Hainan Island Forests - China
33. Andaman Islands Forests - India
34. Sumatran-Nicobar Islands Lowland Forests - Indonesia, India
35. Philippines Moist Forests - Philippines
36. Sumatran Montane Forests - Indonesia
37. Kayah-Karen/Tenasserim Moist Forests - Thailand, Myanmar, Malaysia
38. Peninsular Malaysian Lowland & Montane Forests - Malaysia, Thailand
39. Borneo-Kalimantan Moist Forests - Indonesia, Malaysia
40. Northern Borneo-Palawan Moist Forests - Malaysia, Indonesia, Philippines, Brunei
41. Central Borneo Montane Forests - Indonesia, Malaysia
42. Sulawesi Moist Forests - Indonesia
43. Moluccas Moist Forests - Indonesia
44. Nansei Shoto Archipelago Forests - Japan
Australasia
45. New Guinea Lowland Forests - Papua New Guinea, Indonesia
46. New Guinea Montane Forests - Papua New Guinea, Indonesia
47. New Guinea Outer Islands/Solomons Moist Forests - Papua New Guinea
48. Queensland Tropical Forests - Australia
49. New Caledonia Moist Forests - New Caledonia, France
50. Lord Howe & Norfolk Island Forests - Australia
51. New Zealand Tropical Forests - New Zealand
Oceania
52. South Pacific Islands Forests - Fiji, Samoa, Tonga
53. Hawai'i Moist Forests - United States

TROPICAL & SUBTROPICAL DRY BROADLEAF FORESTS
Neotropical
54. Southern Mexican Dry Forests - Mexico
55. Tumbesian & North Inter-Andean Valleys Dry Forests - Ecuador, Peru, Colombia
56. Bolivian Lowland Dry Forests - Bolivia, Brazil
Afrotropical
57. Macaronesian Forests - Azores, Madeira Islands (Portugal), Canary Islands (Spain), Cape Verde, St. Helena, Ascension (UK)
58. Madagascar Dry Forests - Madagascar
Indo-Malayan
59. Eastern Indian Monsoon Forests - India
60. Eastern Indochina Dry & Monsoon Forests - Vietnam, Laos, Thailand, Cambodia
61. Lesser Sundas Dry & Monsoon Forests - Indonesia
62. New Caledonia Dry Forests - New Caledonia, France
Oceania
63. Hawai'i Dry Forests - United States

TEMPERATE BROADLEAF & MIXED FORESTS
Nearctic
64. Appalachian & Mixed Mesophytic Forests - United States
Palearctic
65. Central China Temperate Forests - China
66. Russian Far East Temperate Forests - Russia, China
67. Eastern Himalayan Broadleaf & Conifer Forests - Bhutan, India, Nepal, Myanmar, China
68. Western Himalayan Temperate Forests - Pakistan, India, Nepal
Indo-Malayan
69. Northeastern India & Myanmar Hill Forests - India, Myanmar
Australasia
70. Eastern Australia Temperate Forests - Australia
71. Tasmanian Temperate Rainforests - Australia
72. South Island Temperate Rainforests - New Zealand

TEMPERATE CONIFEROUS FORESTS
Nearctic
73. Pacific Temperate Rainforests - United States, Canada
74. Klamath-Siskiyou Coniferous Forests - United States
75. Sierra Nevada Conifer Forests - United States
76. Southeastern Conifer & Broadleaf Forests - United States
Neotropical
77. Valdivian Temperate Rainforests - Chile, Argentina
Palearctic
78. Southern European Montane Forests - Bulgaria, Greece, Spain, Italy, France
79. Caucasus & Northeast Anatolia Temperate Forests - Georgia, Azerbaijan, Turkey, Russia, Iran, Armenia
80. Middle Asian Mountains Temperate Forests & Steppe - Kyrgyzstan, Turkmenistan, Afghanistan, Uzbekistan, Kazakstan, Tajikistan, Pakistan, India, Mongolia, China, Iran
81. Altai-Sayan Montane Forests - Russia, Kazakstan, Mongolia, China
82. Mediterranean Conifer Forests - Spain, Italy, Lebanon, Morocco, Algeria, Greece, Turkey, Portugal, France

TROPICAL & SUBTROPICAL CONIFEROUS FORESTS
Neotropical
83. Mexican Pine-Oak Forests - Mexico, United States
84. Greater Antillean Pine Forests - Haiti, Cuba, Dominican Republic

BOREAL FORESTS & TAIGA
Nearctic
85. Northern Cordillera Boreal Forests - Canada
86. Canadian Boreal Taiga - Canada
Palearctic
87. Scandinavian Alpine Tundra & Taiga - Norway, Sweden, Finland
88. Ural Mountains Boreal Forests & Taiga - Russia
89. Central & Eastern Siberian Boreal Forests & Taiga - Russia
90. Kamchatka Boreal Taiga & Grasslands - Russia

TROPICAL & SUBTROPICAL GRASSLANDS, SAVANNAS, & SHRUBLANDS
Neotropical
91. Llanos Savannas - Venezuela, Colombia
92. Cerrado Woodlands & Savannas - Brazil, Bolivia, Paraguay

Afrotropical
93. Sudanian Savannas - Central African Republic, Chad, Uganda, Ethiopia, D.R. Congo, Cameroon, Sudan, Nigeria, Eritrea
94. Horn of Africa Acacia Savannas - Kenya, Somalia, Ethiopia, Eritrea, Sudan
95. East African Acacia Savannas - Kenya, Tanzania, Sudan, Ethiopia, Uganda
96. Central and Eastern Mopane and Miombo - Swaziland, South Africa, Zimbabwe, Botswana, Mozambique, Zambia, Tanzania, Burundi, D.R. Congo, Angola, Malawi, Namibia
Indo-Malayan
97. Terai-Duar Savannas & Grasslands - Nepal, India, Bhutan
Australasia
98. Northern Australia & Trans-Fly Savannas - Australia, Papua New Guinea, Indonesia

TEMPERATE GRASSLANDS, SAVANNAS, & SHRUBLANDS
Nearctic
99. Tallgrass Prairie - United States
Neotropical
100. Patagonian Steppe & Grasslands - Argentina, Chile
Palearctic
101. Daurian Steppe - Mongolia, Russia, China

FLOODED GRASSLANDS & SAVANNAS
Neotropical
102. Everglades Flooded Grasslands - United States
103. Pantanal Flooded Savannas - Bolivia, Brazil, Paraguay
Afrotropical
104. Sahelian Flooded Savannas - Mali, Chad, Niger, Nigeria, Cameroon, Senegal, Mauritania, Sudan, Ethiopia
105. Zambezian Flooded Savannas - Botswana, Namibia, Angola, Zambia, Malawi, Mozambique

MONTANE GRASSLANDS
Neotropical
106. North Andean Paramo - Ecuador, Venezuela, Colombia, Peru
Afrotropical
107. Ethiopian Highlands - Ethiopia, Somalia, Eritrea, Sudan
108. Southern Rift Montane Forests - Malawi, Zimbabwe, Mozambique
109. Angolan Escarpment Woodlands - Angola
110. East African Moorlands - Kenya, Tanzania, Uganda, D.R. Congo, Rwanda
111. Drakensberg Montane Shrublands - South Africa, Lesotho, Swaziland
Indo-Malayan
112. Eastern Himalayan Alpine Meadows - Bhutan, Nepal, India, Myanmar, China
113. Mt. Kinabalu Montane Scrub - Malaysia
Palearctic
114. Tibetan Steppe - China, India

TUNDRA
Nearctic & Palearctic
115. Alaskan North Slope Coastal Tundra - United States, Canada
116. Low Arctic Tundra - Canada
117. Taimyr Tundra - Russia
118. Chukhote Coastal Tundra - Russia

MEDITERRANEAN SHRUB & WOODLANDS
Neotropical
119. California Chaparral & Woodlands - United States, Mexico
120. Chilean Matorral - Chile
Palearctic
121. Mediterranean Shrublands & Woodlands - Portugal, Spain, France, Italy, Monaco, Greece, Yugoslavia, Bosnia and Herzegovina, Croatia, Albania, Turkey, Libya, Lebanon, Israel, Morocco, Algeria, Tunisia, Malta, Cyprus, Macedonia, Bulgaria, Egypt
Afrotropical
122. Fynbos - South Africa
Australasia
123. Southwest Australian Shrublands & Woodlands - Australia

DESERTS & XERIC SHRUBLANDS

Neotropical
124. Sonoran & Baja Deserts - Mexico, United States
125. Chihuahuan & Tehuacán Deserts - Mexico, United States
126. Galápagos Islands Scrubs - Ecuador
127. Atacama Desert - Chile

Afrotropical
128. Seychelles & Mascarene Islands Forests - (e.g., Mauritius, Seychelles, Reunion, Rodrigues)
129. Namib & Karoo Deserts and Shrublands - South Africa, Namibia
130. Kaokoveld Desert - Namibia, Angola
131. Madagascar Spiny Desert - Madagascar
132. Haud-Ogaden Savannas - Somalia
133. Socotra Island Desert - Yemen

Palearctic
134. Arabian Fog and Highland Woodlands & Shrublands - United Arab Emirates, Oman, Yemen, Saudi Arabia
135. Central Asian Sandy Deserts - Turkmenistan, Kazakstan, Uzbekistan, Tajikistan

Australasia
136. Carnavon Xeric Scrubs - Australia
137. Great Sandy Deserts & Central Ranges - Australia, Tasmania

FRESHWATER ECOREGIONS
SMALL RIVERS & STREAMS

Nearctic
138. Mississippi Piedmont Rivers & Streams - United States
139. Southeastern Rivers & Streams - United States
140. Pacific Northwest Coastal Rivers & Streams - United States
141. Gulf of Alaska Coastal Rivers & Streams - United States, Canada

Neotropical
142. Guyanan Highlands Freshwater Ecosystems - Venezuela, Brazil, Guyana, Colombia
143. Greater Antillean Streams - Cuba, Jamaica, Haiti, Dominican Republic
144. Upper Amazon & Orinoco Rivers & Streams - Ecuador, Venezuela, Colombia, Peru, Brazil, Bolivia
145. Upper Paraná- Brazil, Paraguay, Argentina

Afrotropical
146. Upper Guinea Rivers and Streams - Guinea, Sierra Leone, Côte d'Ivoire, Ghana
147. Madagascar Freshwater Ecosystems - Madagascar
148. Gulf of Guinea Rivers & Crater Lakes - Gabon, Equatorial Guinea, Cameroon, Togo, Nigeria, Benin, R. Congo, D.R. Congo, Central African Republic, Ghana
149. Congo Basin Piedmont Rivers & Streams - D.R. Congo, R. Congo, Angola, Central African Republic, Zambia
150. Cape Rivers and Streams - South Africa

Indo-Malayan
151. Southwestern Sri Lanka Rivers & Streams - Sri Lanka
152. Sundaland Rivers & Swamps - Malaysia, Indonesia, Brunei
153. Western Ghats Rivers & Streams - India

Palearctic
154. Balkan Rivers and Streams - Greece, Italy, Yugoslavia, Bosnia-Herzegovina, Croatia, Albania, Macedonia, Bulgaria, Slovenia
155. East Anatolian Rivers and Streams - Turkey
156. Xi Jiang Rivers and Streams - China, Vietnam
157. Russian Far East Rivers & Wetlands - Russia, China

Australasia
158. New Guinea Rivers & Streams - Papua New Guinea, Indonesia
159. New Caledonia Rivers & Streams - New Caledonia, France
160. Kimberley Rivers & Streams - Australia
161. Southwest Australia Rivers & Streams - Australia
162. Eastern Australia Rivers & Streams - Australia

LARGE RIVERS

Nearctic
163. Colorado River - United States, Mexico

Neotropical
164. Varzea & Igapó Freshwater Ecosystems - Brazil, Peru, Colombia, Venezuela
165. Brazilian Shield Amazonian Rivers & Streams - Brazil, Bolivia

Afrotropical
166. Congo River - D.R. Congo, R. Congo, Angola

Indo-Malayan
167. Mekong & Salween Rivers - Cambodia, Vietnam, Laos, Myanmar, Thailand, China
168. Yangtze River & Lakes - China

LAKE & CLOSED BASIN FRESHWATER ECOSYSTEMS

Neotropical
169. Chihuahuan Rivers & Springs - Mexico, United States
170. Mexican Highland Lakes - Mexico
171. High Andean Lakes - Chile, Bolivia, Argentina, Peru

Afrotropical
172. Rift Valley Lakes - D.R. Congo, Uganda, Ethiopia, Tanzania, Kenya, Rwanda, Malawi, Mozambique, Burundi, Zambia

Palearctic
173. Lake Baikal - Russia
174. Yunnan Lakes & Streams - China
175. Lake Biwa - Japan

Indo-Malayan
176. Palawan & Mindanao Streams & Lakes (Lake Lanao) - Philippines
177. Lake Inle - Myanmar
178. Central Sulawesi Lakes - Indonesia

Australasia
179. Lakes Kutubu & Sentani - Papua New Guinea, Indonesia

MARINE ECOREGIONS
LARGE DELTAS, MANGROVES, & ESTUARIES

Nearctic
180. Chesapeake Bay & Delaware Bay - United States

Neotropical
181. Central American Mangroves - Belize, Mexico, Honduras, Nicaragua, El Salvador, Panama, Guatémala, Costa Rica
182. Panama Bight Mangroves - Ecuador, Panama, Colombia
183. Orinoco-Amazon Mangroves & Coastal Swamps - Venezuela, Trinidad & Tobago, Guyana, Suriname, French Guiana, Brazil
184. Mexican Mangroves - Mexico

Afrotropical
185. Senegal & Gambia River Mangroves & Wetlands - Senegal, Gambia, Guinea, Guinea-Bissau
186. Guinean-Congolian Coast Mangroves - Nigeria, Cameroon, Benin, Togo, Ghana, R. Congo, Ivory Coast, Liberia, Equatorial Guinea, Gabon, Sierra Leone, São Tomé & Príncipe, D.R. Congo
187. East African Mangroves - Kenya, Tanzania, Somalia, Mozambique

Palearctic
188. Volga River Delta - Russia, Kazakstan
189. Mesopotamian Delta & Marshes - Iraq, Iran, Kuwait
190. Danube River Delta - Romania, Ukraine, Moldavia
191. Lena River Delta - Russia

Indo-Malayan
192. Mekong River Delta Mangroves - Vietnam, Cambodia
193. Sundarbans Mangroves - India, Bangladesh
194. Sundaland & Eastern Indonesian Archipelago Mangroves - Indonesia
195. Indus River Delta & Rann of Kutch - Pakistan, India

Australasia
196. New Guinea Mangroves - Papua New Guinea, Indonesia

CORAL REEF & ASSOCIATED MARINE ECOSYSTEMS

Western Atlantic
197. Mesoamerican Reef - Belize, Guatemala, Honduras, Mexico
198. Southern Caribbean Sea - Panama, Colombia, Venezuela, Trinidad & Tobago, Netherlands Antilles
199. Greater Antilles & Bahamian Marine Ecosystems - Jamaica, Cuba, Haiti, Dominican Republic, Cayman Islands, Bahamas, United States, Turks & Caicos

Western Indian Ocean
200. East African and Madagascar Marine Ecosystems - Kenya, Tanzania, Mozambique, Somalia, Madagascar

201. Red Sea Marine Ecosystems - Egypt, Israel, Saudi Arabia, Yemen, Eritrea, Djibouti, Sudan, Jordan
202. Agulhas Current Marine Ecosystems - Mozambique, South Africa

Northern Indian Ocean
203. Arabian Sea & Persian Gulf - Bahrain, Saudi Arabia, United Arab Emirates, Qatar, Oman, Iraq, Iran, Pakistan, Kuwait, Yemen
204. Maldives, Lakshadweep, & Chagos Marine Ecosystems - Maldives, India, United Kingdom

Eastern Indian Ocean
205. Western Australian Marine Ecosystems - Australia

Western Pacific Ocean
206. Nansei Shoto Marine Ecosystems - Japan
207. Sulu Sea - Philippines, Malaysia
208. Sulawesi Sea - Philippines, Indonesia, Malaysia
209. Banda-Flores Seas Marine Ecosystems - Indonesia
210. Northern New Guinea & Coral Sea Marine Ecosystems - Papua New Guinea, Indonesia, Solomon Islands
211. Micronesian Marine Ecosystems - Palau, Federated States of Micronesia

Eastern Pacific Ocean
212. Panama Bight Marine Ecosystems - Panama, Colombia, Ecuador

Southern Pacific Ocean
213. South Pacific Marine Ecosystems - Vanuatu, Fiji, New Caledonia, France, Tonga, Tuvalu, Niue, Wallis & Futuna, Western Samoa, American Samoa
214. Great Barrier Reef - Australia
215. Eastern Polynesian Island Marine Ecosystems - (particularly, Hawai'i, Marquesas, Easter Island, Societies & Tuamotus)
216. Lord Howe Island & Norfolk Island Marine Ecosystems - Australia

COASTAL MARINE ECOSYSTEMS

Northern Atlantic Ocean
217. Icelandic & Celtic Marine Ecosystems - Iceland, France, Ireland, United Kingdom
218. Grand Banks - Canada, United States
219. Wadden Sea - Denmark, Germany, Belgium, The Netherlands

Western Atlantic Ocean
220. Northeast Brazilian Coast Marine Ecosystems - Brazil

Eastern Atlantic Ocean
221. Gulf of Guinea Marine Ecosystems - Equatorial Guinea, Gabon, R. Congo, D.R. Congo, Angola, Cameroon, Nigeria, Benin, Togo, São Tomé & Príncipe
222. Western Guinea Current Marine Ecosystems - Senegal, Gambia, Guinea-Bissau, Guinea, Sierra Leone, Cape Verde, Liberia, Mauritania

Southern Atlantic Ocean
223. Benguela Current - Namibia, South Africa, Angola
224. Southwest Atlantic Coast Marine Ecosystems - Argentina, Uruguay, Brazil

Mediterranean Sea
225. Mediterranean Sea

Western Pacific Ocean
226. Yellow Sea & East China Sea - China, North Korea, South Korea, Japan

Eastern Pacific Ocean
227. Californian Current - United States, Canada, Mexico
228. Sea of Cortez - Mexico
229. Peru Current - Peru, Chile
230. Galápagos Islands Marine Ecosystems - Ecuador
231. Magellanic Marine Ecosystems - Chile, Argentina

Southern Pacific Ocean
232. South Temperate Australian Marine Ecosystems - Australia

POLAR & SUBPOLAR MARINE ECOSYSTEMS

Antarctic Seas
233. Antarctic Peninsula & Weddell Sea
234. New Zealand Marine Ecosystems - New Zealand

Arctic Ocean & Seas
235. Bering & Beaufort Seas - Russia, United States, Canada
236. Sea of Okhotsk & Northern Sea of Japan - Russia, Japan
237. Svalbard/Franz Joseph Land Marine Ecosystems - Russia, Norway

INDEX

Page numbers of photographs are in italics.